The Small Business Guide (U.S.)

2013 Edition

This publication is designed to provide information regarding the subject matter covered. It is sold with the understanding that the author is not rendering professional services. If legal, marketing, financial, or any other expert assistance is required, the services of a competent professional person should be sought.

Edited by Latasia D. Brown

Includes Index
ISBN 978-0-982-9036-9-8

Library of Congress Control Number: 2011960117

Printed in the United States of America

CONTENTS

Introduction

Are you someone seeking to start your own business and frustrated with the lack of straightforward answers to your countless questions? *Or* are you a business owner whose time is too consumed with researching how to spark growth instead of actually *performing* the right actions that spur growth and success? *Or* is there an entrepreneur *inside of you* that isn't given the chance to come out because you don't know where to start and the prospect seems too complicated to even fathom?

If any or all of the above describes your situation then you've opened the right book. Every year millions of new businesses are started in the United States, and yet there is no single informative source where people can turn to in order to find answers to basic questions the future entrepreneur will be faced with.

In this high-tech world of information overload finding the information you must have to succeed in business in a timely and concise manner can be a daunting task. We have decided to save you the headache and do your homework for you.

The Small Business Guide will walk you through the entire journey of building your own business from the ground up. The idea of creating a conglomerate of your own, successfully, may be an intimidating thought simply because it isn't that simple. This guide breaks down the most difficult tasks and possible future obstacles so that producing success from scratch becomes simply simple.

Now don't get us wrong, there will be blood, sweat and tears involved – more sweat than anything else. But now you have the best tools and the right answers at your fingertips.

Put your doubts, fears and anxieties aside, and go forth and be profitable!

CHAPTER 1

IS IT A BUSINESS?

There is a central question future Entrepreneurs should ask themselves: Am I creating a business or a job?

Don't let your startup business or home-based business become a home-based job. It's not a business if the enterprise is only generating a small amount of money with no growth potential where you could earn enough money to hire new employees, or if the operation comes to a halt when you are out sick or on vacation and can't continue to earn money for you.

A business is an entity that continues to function and generate income in your absence. This means that you have to grow the business from a "one-person" operation to the point of hiring employees who can continue the functions of what you established even while you are away. When creating a business you must have realistic expectations about income and growth. Projected earnings of only $50,000 per year will not be enough to pay the salary of more than one individual (the owner) and cover all other costs such as rent, production cost, utilities, business insurance, health insurance, etc. You cannot take on new employees on a business income like that.

Build growth by doing things that bring in more work, more clients and generates more demand for your products or services. This means that you have to advertise and produce more to meet the demand for your goods and/or services. As a result you will achieve greater income and be able to hire employees who can do the work and continue the functions of the business even when you're away.

CHAPTER 2

A SIMPLE PLAN

So, you have an idea about the type of business you want to start. Where do you go from there? The next step is to create a **simple plan**.

It's not necessary to have an elaborate formal business plan to go into business *(formal business plans for the most part are used to obtain financing from Venture Capitalists or other financial institutions)*. Think of a simple plan as a roadmap that shows the major roadways and key features as opposed to the formal business plan that shows street level details.

To arrive at your **simple plan** engage in some **backwards planning** by answering a few questions. **Backwards planning** is starting at the end and working your way back to the beginning. Start with outlining what it is that you want to achieve and working step-by-step back to the beginning (**See a sample "Simple Plan" at Appendix A**).

CHAPTER 3

SEQUENTIAL STEPS FOR FORMING A BUSINESS

Get your business started by following these simple steps:

1. **PICK A BUSINESS NAME:** The name should give an indication as to the nature of the business. It should be unique and easy to remember. Check with the state in which you intend to register the name to verify that it is not already taken. You should also do some research on the Web.

2. **GET THE DOMAIN NAME REGISTERED:** Research the name on the Internet and ensure that it is not already taken. If it's not taken, register the domain name. Your Web site name and the e-mail account information you put on your business card should reflect your business name. That is why it's important to register your business name as your domain name. For example, the business name is **Red Flowers; Inc.** therefore you should register your domain name as **www.redflowers.com**.

3. **OBTAIN A PROFESSIONAL LICENSE OR PERMIT IF REQUIRED:** Some businesses require a "Professional License" or "Permit" in order to operate legally. This differs from state to state. Click on the link to find out more.

4. **FIND A LOCATION FOR THE BUSINESS:** Once you start registering your business with the states they will ask for the business address. You want to have this ready.

5. **DETERMINE THE TYPE OF ORGANIZATION:** Determine how the business will be organized, i.e., sole proprietorship, partnership, corporation, etc.

6. **DETERMINE WHERE YOU WANT TO REGISTER THE BUSINESS:** Choose between a State Corporation, Delaware Corporation or a Nevada Corporation.

7. **REGISTER THE BUSINESS:** If you've decided on a **state** entity register the business with the respective state. If you decided

to go with a **Delaware** or **Nevada Corporation** register with those respective entities. However, if you register as a Delaware or Nevada Corporation and you will be selling products or have a presence (office) in other states, you must also register with those states as a **"Foreign Corporation."** This applies also if you register your business in one state and will sell products or maintain a presence (office) in other states. Once the business is registered with the respective state it is legal for you to operate as a business entity within that state.

8. OBTAIN A FEIN (FEDERAL EMPLOYER IDENTIFICATION NUMBER) FROM THE IRS: This is the tax ID that identifies you as a business entity with the federal government for the purpose of paying taxes.

9. REGISTER THE BUSINESS WITH THE COUNTY: You have to file a copy of your incorporation papers with the respective county in which the business is located.

10. OBTAIN A SALES TAX ID FROM THE STATE: If you are selling goods you have to obtain a sales tax ID from the state, which establishes an account for the business to pay sales taxes.

11. OBTAIN A BUSINESS LICENSE FROM THE LOCAL MUNICIPALITY: You have to obtain a business license from the city or township in which the business is located. A business license makes it legal for your business to operate in the respective city or township.

CHAPTER 4

BUSINESS IDEAS

To start a business you first need a good idea. Ideas for starting a new business are all around you. These are some questions to consider when trying to find ideas for starting a business:

1.   Ask yourself, what do you need in your home that is not on the market?

Products in the home such as the can opener, the salt and pepper shaker, the blender, the bed, the TV, the remote control, the Clapper way of turning lights on and off, are all inventions that people came up with to fulfill a need in the home. That does not mean that everything that is needed in the home has already been invented, quite the opposite. People are coming up with new ideas for inventions every day. You probably have a few ideas of your own. Pursue them!

2.   What do kids need that is not on the market?

I saw a TV show where someone had an idea for turning a regular baby carriage into a rocking chair by putting the wheel of the baby carriage into a device that moves the chair back and forth. He had this idea for 35 years and is just now patenting it and putting it on the market. The idea not only solved a problem he saw when his kids were born, but also solves the one he now has with the birth of his grandchild. Someone recently came up with a vest that you wear which has pockets to store baby items in. Parents are in a great position to observe their kids and identify solutions to some of their problems. Take advantage of the unique opportunity you have and pursue the idea when you think of a solution to a problem.

3.   What is missing from your neighborhood?

Do you live in an area that does not have a restaurant, car wash, car repair shop, ice cream shop, pizza shop, barber shop, beauty salon, massage parlor, computer repair shop, cyber cafe, coffee shop, laundry, cleaners, etc.? If you live in a location with a reasonable size population and yet people have to travel great distances to utilize those services, then think of it as a business opportunity. People would rather shop and take care of their personal needs closer to home rather than travel long distances to obtain basic necessities. What is the ethnic makeup of your neighborhood? Your business could be, "providing tailored services that satisfy their needs."

4.   What items would make it better for you to complete a task that is not yet on the market?

You're working on a project and you suddenly find yourself saying, "I could do this much more efficiently if I had 'X'." Well, why don't you be the person to invent "X" and bring it to the market? Why wait for someone else to do it? We all share the common experience of asking where is "X"...how come no one has invented "X" yet; time to stop asking and start doing.

5.   How often have you heard your friends or colleagues at work say "I wish something like that exist."

If someone is telling you that they wished that something like "that" existed take it as a clue that there is a market for "that." Chances are pretty good that there are thousands or millions of people asking for the same thing. Get a move on it before someone else beat you to it!

6. Is there a better way?
1.   How often have you gone by a business (a salon, grocery store, repair shop, etc.) and noticed that the business was not succeeding? How often have you frequented by a business and said to your-self, "if they did this or that, they could be successful?" Just because an idea has been already attempted does not mean that it cannot be tried again more successfully. If you see something that's been done before, but you think that there is a better way of doing it, why not give it a try? Just because someone is the first to do something it does not mean that they are guaranteed success. He who does it better will be successful.

7. Do you watch TV shows that showcase entrepreneurs?

A great way to get business ideas and stimulate entrepreneurial thinking is to watch TV shows that showcase entrepreneurs like the following:

MAKING IT TV:
(http://www.makingittv.com/streamingvideodomain.htm): This is a video streamed over the Internet that showcases interviews with small business owners. Follow the link above to see the show.

THE SHARK TANK:
(http://abc.go.com/shows/shark-tank/about-the-show): This is a show that airs on ABC. The show gives entrepreneurs to make a pitch to Venture Capitalists and convince them to invest in their business. Visit the website above to find the time and dates for the airing of show.

The ENTREPRENEURS:
(http://www.cnbc.com/id/26565293) - This show airs on CNBC. You can also view it online. It showcases entrepreneurs who have achieved success and gives them the opportunity to tell their story.

CHAPTER 5

YOU HAVE AN IDEA FOR A BUSINESS, NOW WHAT?

If you have a unique idea for a business you should take every measure to protect it. Ideas can become intellectual property and thus valuable assets. Intellectual property can be protected in one of three ways: **patent, trademark** or **copyright**.

Patent, trademark or copyright provides legal protection of your ideas. If you have ideas for businesses you want to pursue you should consider these options before proceeding. If you do not have legal protection for your ideas it is possible for someone to steal those ideas from you.

Not all ideas can be protected by these measures, however, many can.

What is a Patent?

A patent grants you the exclusive right to your idea, while excluding others from making, using, offering for sale or selling the invention for a limited period of time (20 years for Utility patent and 14 years for Plant patent).

There are three types of patents, **utility, plant** and **design** patents.

Utility Patents:
Utility patents are issued for the invention of a new and useful process, machine, manufacture or composition of matter or a new and useful improvement thereof.

Plant Patents:
Plant patents are issued for new and <u>distinct</u>, invented or discovered asexually reproduced plant.

Design Patents:
Design patents are issued for new, original and ornamental designs for an article of manufacture.

You can file for a patent by using a patent attorney or you can learn the process and attempt to do it yourself. The use of patent attorneys will cost a minimum of $2,000.

You can file a provisional patent application if you want to start getting protection for your idea before you are ready to file a patent. A provisional patent only requires a written description and any drawings that describe the invention. You must file a full patent within 12 months.

You can find patent attorneys by visiting the USPTO Web site at: **https://oedci.uspto.gov/OEDCI/**

The filing of a non-provisional application with the Patent and Trademark Office will cost a minimum of $515.

The filing fee for a provisional application is $105.

There are additional *issue* and *maintenance* fees associated with patents. Plant and design patents require no maintenance fee.

The average time to get a patent approved is two years.

To learn more about patents visit the USPTO Web site at: **http://www.uspto.gov/web/offices/com/iip/patents.htm# Patent**

What is a Trademark?
A trademark is a word, phrase, symbol or design, or a combination of words, phrases, symbols or designs that identifies and distinguishes the source of the goods of one party from those of others. For example, the company's logo, the company's name and the name of a product can be trademarked.

Filing for a trademark is a simple process. This can be done without the use of an attorney. However, if you need the advice of an attorney you should seek it.

The fee for filing a trademark application depends on the number of class you want to register the mark for. The minimum fee is $275.

It could take one to several years to complete the trademark registration process depending on the legal issues that may arise in the examination of the application.

Learn more about trademarks from the USPTO Web site at: **http://www.uspto.gov/index.html#**

What is a Copyright?
Copyright offers legal protection against all kinds of works such as written documents, software, music, video, etc. It gives you legal protection in the event that someone else reproduces and distributes your work without your permission.

Copyright registration is managed by the Library of Congress.

You can submit your application without the use of an attorney. You simply fill out the PDF application form, print it and mail it along with your work.

The cost to file a copyright application starts at **$35**. Be sure to use the correct form when filing.

Works protected under copyright laws lasts long after the life of the author.

It takes an average of nine months to complete the process.

Answers to questions such as what is a copyright, what is protected and what is not, etc. can be found at:
http://www.copyright.gov/help/faq

CHAPTER 6

BUSINESS MODELING

A business model is the methods by which a company intends to generate revenues and become profitable. It defines the manner by which the business enterprise delivers value to customers, entices customers to pay for value, and converts those payments to profit. A business model can be simple or complex.
These are some well-known business models. You are probably familiar with some of them. To better illustrate this point let's examine the examples below.

Bricks Business Model: This is when a company sell products from a retail location. Customers come into the store and make purchases. The sales transaction takes place at the retail site and the customer walks out the door with the product.

Clicks Business Model: This is when a company sell products through a website. Customers go to the website and place an order and the product is delivered to the customer at their place of business or residence via the mail service.

Bricks and Clicks Business Model: This is when a company integrates both offline (bricks) and online (clicks) presence. For example, a store allows customers to order products through their website, but lets them pick up the product at a local store.

Direct Sales Business Model: Direct selling is marketing and selling products to consumers directly. There is no retail location or website location where customers can place orders and pickup the products. Sales are made through one-on-one interactions between the seller and the customer. This is done through demonstrations, private parties (in homes or place of business), and other private arrangements.

Cutting out the Middle Man Business Model: In many industries the traditional way to get to your customers is to go through an intermediary such as distributor, wholesaler, broker, or agent. In this model you will bypass the intermediaries and sell directly to your customers. A good example of this is the service provided by amazon.com and Printers that let authors become publishers by printing and selling their own books to directly customers without going through Publishers and Distributors.

Franchise Business Model: This is the type of arrangement whereby the cost of establishing and running individual business locations is shared by the owner (franchisor) and an investor (franchisee). They share in the cost and profits of the business but the franchisee will have greater liability for his part of the chain. The franchisee has a greater incentive than a direct employee because he/she has a direct stake in the business.

Other business models include, Multi-level Marketing, Loyalty, Auction, Online Auction, Pyramid, etc.

You don't have to confine yourself to the traditional models. You can devise your own business model. See other examples and get some idea on how you can model your business to achieve success by going to *http://www.s-b-z.com* (under Business Modeling).

CHAPTER 7

FORMING THE BUSINESS

WHO CAN FORM A BUSINESS IN THE UNITED STATES

The following can incorporate a business:
- One or more individual(s) (U.S. or foreign residents)
- An organization (domestic or foreign)
- Must be of legal age (18 years of age or older)

AGE REQUIREMENT FOR FORMING A BUSINESS

The age requirement for forming a corporation varies from state to state. Most states require that the incorporator be at least 18 years of age, while other states have not established a minimum age limit. States that have not established a legal age still require that the individual be of legal age required to enter into contracts (which is 18 years old in most states).

An individual does not have to be a resident of the state in order to incorporate in that state.

WHAT IS A FOREIGN CORPORATION

A foreign corporation is a business that was incorporated in one state or overseas and conducts business in another.

For example, BBZ Co. is incorporated in Arizona, but also conducts business in California. In Arizona it is considered a domestic corporation, and in California it is considered a foreign entity.

If a business is incorporated in one state or overseas and wishes to do business in another state then it must be registered with the respective state as a foreign entity.

Many states require that foreign entities use a register agent in order to register their business. The register agent must be authorized by and reside in the respective state.

DETERMINE THE TYPE OF ORGANIZATION

When organizing a new business, one of the most important decisions to be made is choosing the structure of your operation.

The form in which you conduct your business determines issues such as the extent of personal liability that you have from the business and how the business will be taxed. If you are uncertain about your choice you should consult with an accountant and an attorney to help you select the form of ownership that is right for you.

The most common forms of business organizations include:

> **Sole Proprietorship**
> **Partnership**
> **General Partnership**
> **Limited Partnership**
> **Limited Liability Partnership**
> **Corporation**
> **Subchapter S Corporation**
> **Subchapter C Corporation**
> **Limited Liability Company**

SOLE PROPRIETOR:

The vast majority of small businesses start out as sole proprietorships. These firms are owned by one person, usually the individual who possesses the day to day responsibilities for running the business. Sole proprietors own all the assets and profits generated the business. They also assume "complete personal" responsibility for all of its liabilities or debts. In the eyes of the law you are one in the same with the business. Hence, you are personally responsible for any liabilities the business may incur. This is different from a corporation which protects you and your personal assets from the liability of the corporation. Although you're not required to register with the IRS it is necessary in most states. A sole proprietor may do business with their own name or with a trade name other than his or her legal name. In most states the sole proprietor is required to register the trade name or "Doing Business As" (DBA) name -- that is if you are doing business as a name other than your own. This also allows the proprietor to open a business account with banking institutions.

Visit the IRS sole proprietorship information page to learn more.
http://www.irs.gov/businesses/small/article/0,,id=98202,00 .html

Advantages:
1. **Ease of Setup:** Easiest and least expensive form of ownership to organize.
2. **Single Control:** Sole proprietors are in complete control, within the law, to make all decisions.
3. **Income:** Sole proprietors receive all income generated by the business to keep or reinvest.
4. **No Double Taxation:** Profits from the business flow-through directly to the owner's personal tax return.
5. **Dissolution:** If desired, the business is easy to dissolve.

Disadvantages:
1. **Unlimited liability:** You are legally responsible for all debts and actions against the business. Your business and personal assets are 100% at risk.
2. **Financing**: Financial institutions find it difficult to lend to this type of business because of the high-risk factor. Hence you are limited to using funds from personal savings or consumer loans.
3. **Growth:** Have a hard time attracting high-caliber employees, or those that are motivated by the opportunity to own a part of the business.

PARTNERSHIP:
A contract between two or more persons (such as a corporation and an individual or two individuals) who agree to pool talent and money and share profits or losses. Partnerships can be **general** or **limited**. Crucial to the functioning of a partnership is a **Partnership agreement.** It is strongly advised to draw up a Partnership agreement up front with your partners that address how the organization will be run and the roles and responsibilities

of all the partners involved. This will eliminate sticky problems down the road.

In terms of asset protection, general partnerships can be worse than sole proprietorships. What one partner does have an effect on all of the partners because each partner of the general partnership is personally responsible for all obligations of the partnership. Thus, each general partner's exposure to risk is increased by a factor equal to the number of general partners in the business.

Partnership taxation is codified as Subchapter K of Chapter 1 of the U.S. Internal Revenue Code (Title 26 of the United States Code).

Partnerships are "flow-through" entities for United States federal income taxation purposes. Flow-through taxation means that the entity does not pay taxes on its income. Instead, the owners of the entity pay tax on their "distributive share" of the entity's taxable income, even if no funds are distributed by the partnership to the owners. Federal tax law permits the owners of the entity to agree how the income of the entity will be allocated among them.

A partnership must file an annual information return to report the income, deductions, gains, losses, etc., from its operations, but it does not pay income tax.

Partners are not employees and should not be issued a Form W-2.

The partnership must furnish copies of Schedule K-1 (Form 1065) to the partners by the date Form 1065 is required to be filed, including extensions. Partnerships are still required to deposit employee taxes and pay Federal Unemployment Tax and deposit Social Security and Medicare taxes.

Learn more about partnerships from the IRS partnership webpage: **http://www.irs.gov/businesses/small/article/0,,id=98214,00 .html**

Below is a list of Web addresses where you can find sample partnership agreements. *Visit The Small Business Zone Web site (**http://www.sbz1.com**) for a more extensive list.*

Better Investing Community
http://legacy.betterinvesting.org/articles/web/3462

Find Law
http://smallbusiness.findlaw.com/business-forms-contracts/business-forms-contracts-a-to-z/form4-1.html

Law Smart
http://www.lawsmart.com/documents/partnership_agreement.shtml

Advantages:

1. **Ease of formation:** Some states don't require registration.
2. **Low start up costs:** Each partner can contribute startup cost thus reducing individual contributions.
3. **Additional sources of investment:** A partnership can obtain new investment sources by taking on more partners who are willing to invest in the organization.
4. **Possible tax advantage:** Partners are taxed at their individual personal income rate. The partnership does not pay a corporate income tax.
5. **Limited regulation:** Some states don't regulate partnerships.
6. **Broader management base:** Partnerships can rely on the broad management experience of its partners to run he business instead of a single individual.

Disadvantages:

1. **Unlimited liability:** The owners are personally liable for any legal actions and financial debts the organization may incur.
2. **Lack of continuity in business:** If a partner decides to leave, the partnership will cease to exist.
3. **Organization in absence of owner:** Ownership is shared between the partners; there is no single owner.
4. **Difficulty in raising capital:** Financial institutions find it difficult to lend to an organization that does not have perpetual existence and to which the members are exposed to great risks.

GENERAL PARTNERSHIP:

This is a partnership in which each partner is liable for all partnership debts and obligations regardless of the amount of the individual partner's capital contribution. General partners are those who are responsible for the day-to-day management of activities, whose individual acts are binding on all the partners, and who are personally responsible for the partnership's total liabilities.

Crucial to the functioning of a partnership is a Partnership Agreement. It is strongly advised to draw up a Partnership Agreement up front with your partners that address how the organization will be run and the roles and responsibilities of all partners. This will eliminate sticky problems down the road.

Advantages:
1. **Ease of formation:** Some states don't require registration.
2. **Low Cost start up:** Each partner contributes to the startup cost thus reducing individual contributions.
3. **Tax advantage:** The owners of the entity pay tax on their "distributive share" of the entity's taxable income.

Disadvantages:
1. Each partner has unlimited liability.
2. **Lack of continuity:** The organization could suffer if a partner pulls out.
3. No single owner.

LIMITED PARTNERSHIP:

A limited partnership is one consisting of both **General** and **Limited Partners**.

General Partner(s) have management control, share the right to use partnership property, share the profits of the firm in predefined proportions and have joint and several liability for the debts of the partnership. As in a general partnership, the General Partners have actual authority as agents of the firm to bind all the other partners in contracts with third parties that are in the ordinary course of the partnership's business. **General Partner(s)** collects fees and a percentage of the capital gains and income.

Limited Partners invest money but have limited liability, are not involved in day-to-day management and usually cannot lose more than their capital contribution. Usually **Limited Partners** receive income, capital gains and tax benefits. The extent of their income is normally spelled out in a partnership agreement. Limited Partners are like shareholders in a corporation.

Limited partnerships are distinct from limited liability partnerships, in which all partners have limited liability.

Advantages:
1. **Limited Liability:** Limited Partners have limited liability.
2. **Financing:** Additional sources of revenue can be achieved by bringing in other limited partners.

Disadvantages:
1. **Liability:** General partners have full liability.
2. **Lack of continuity:** The organization could cease to exist if a partner pulls out if not properly addressed in a partnership agreement.

LIMITED LIABILITY PARTNERSHIP:
Business entity that has limited liability for all partners (except for professional negligence of each). Just like shareholders in a corporation. A hybrid form of organization in which all partners enjoy limited liability for the business's debts. It combines the limited liability advantage of a corporation with the tax advantages of a partnership.

However, unlike corporate shareholders, the partners have the right to manage the business directly.

Partners of a limited liability partnership are not liable for other partners' (or employee or agent of the partnership) negligence, malpractice or wrongful acts or misconduct. However, they are liable for other partnership debts and obligations as well as for their own negligence, malpractice, wrongful acts or misconduct and that of any person under their direct supervision and control.

If there is no partnership agreement, income, losses and gains will be allocated in proportion to the partnership interests of each partner. Partners can agree among themselves as to how income, losses and gains are divided among the partners. The partners then report the amount allocated on their own income tax returns and pay tax accordingly.

A limited liability partnership ("LLP") is essentially the same thing as a **limited liability company** ("LLC"), except that an LLP is **specifically designed for use by certain professions** (for example: accountants, lawyers and architects).

Advantages:
1. **Pass-Through Taxation:** Income, losses and gains are passed through to the partners according to the partnership agreement and reported as personal income.
2. **Lower Tax Rate:** Partners are taxed at the personal tax rate rather than at the corporate tax rate.
3. **Limited Liability:** All partners are not held personally responsible for the debts and liabilities of the business.
4. **Partnership conversion:** Easier conversion from a general partnership to an LLP than to a LLC or corporation.

Disadvantages:
1. **Liability:** Partners are still exposed to some degree of liability.
2. **Lack of continuity in business:** If a partner decides to leave, the partnership may cease to exist. You must specify in the partnership agreement how this situation will be handled in order to maintain continuity of the organization.
3. **Organization in absence of owner:** Ownership is shared between the partners. There is no single owner.
4. **Difficulty in raising capital:** Financial institutions find it difficult to lend to an organization that does not have perpetual existence and to which the members are exposed to some degree of risk.

CORPORATION:

A corporation is a group of people granted a charter legally recognizing them as a separate entity having its own rights, powers, privileges and liabilities distinct and separate from those of its members. An artificial entity created under and governed by the Laws of the state of incorporation. It's also a legal entity, which can own property, incur debts, sue and be sued. Corporations provide limited liability, easy transfer of ownership and continuity of existence.

Ownership is held by stockholders who have limited liability. A corporation can be a **STOCK** or a **NON STOCK** corporation.. The two main types of corporations are **For-Profit** and **Non-Profit**.

There are three types of For-Profit Corporations, *S Corporations*, *C Corporations* and *Limited Liability Corporations*. Generally, a corporation files **Articles of Incorporation** with the state, laying out the general nature of the corporation, the amount of stock it is authorized to issue and the names and addresses of directors. Once the articles are approved the corporation's directors meet to create **bylaws** that govern the internal functions of the corporation such as meeting procedures and officer positions.
 The law of the jurisdiction in which a corporation operates will regulate most of its internal activities, as well as its finances. If a corporation operates outside its home state, it is often required to register with other governments as a **foreign corporation,** and is almost always subject to laws of its host state pertaining to employment, crimes, contracts, civil actions and the like.

Corporations are required to file and pay tax on a regular basis (such as quarterly) depending on the nature of the tax (for example, unemployment insurance tax, sales tax, corporate income tax, etc.)

Residual Interest: Members of a corporation (except for non-profit corporations) are said to have a "residual interest." Should the corporation end its existence, the members are the last to receive its assets, following creditors and others with interests in the corporation.

Visit the IRS' corporation Web page to learn more:
http://www.irs.gov/businesses/small/article/0,,id=98359,00
.html

Advantages:
1. **Limited Liability:** Stockholders are protected from any criminal or financial liability the corporation incurs apart from their investment.
2. **Ownership is transferable:** Ownership is transferable through the transfer of stocks.
3. **Continuous existence:** The organization does not cease to exist if the owner dies. Corporations can continue to live from generation to generation.

Disadvantages:
1. **Closely regulated:** States and federal laws govern the formation and operation of corporations, and the U.S. Corporations have to abide by several legal requirements.
2. **Most expensive to organize:** Costs incurred from hiring a Board of Directors, paying for the annual Board of Directors meeting and the annual stockholders meeting. There are legal and professional fees (such as accountant fees), etc.
3. **Extensive record keeping:** Corporations must create bylaws and maintain the records of the meetings of the Board of Directors and the stockholders.
4. **Diluted ownership:** Ownership is represented by the number of stocks owned. Someone with a majority of stock ownership has greater control of the company. Each stock represents a vote.
5. **Double taxation:** The Corporation's income is taxed at the corporate rate and the dividend paid to stockholders is taxed as capital gains.

SUBCHAPTER S CORPORATION:

An S Corporation ("S Corp.") is an ordinary business corporation that has elected to be taxed under Subchapter S of the Internal Revenue Code. It is not taxed on its earnings as a corporation, but instead its earnings are passed to its shareholders for tax purposes. However, an S Corp. has certain limits on the number of shareholders it may have and who may be shareholders is limited to one class of stock and has to operate under a group of other rules.

Some states, such as New York and New Jersey, require a separate state-level 'S' election in order for the corporation to be treated as an S corporation, for state tax purposes.

If a corporation meets the foregoing requirements and wishes to be taxed under Subchapter S, its shareholders may file Form 2553.

If a corporation that has elected to be treated as an S corporation ceases to meet the requirements (for example, if as a result of stock transfers, the number of shareholders exceeds 100 or an ineligible shareholder such as a nonresident alien acquires a share), the Corporation will lose its S corporation status and revert to being a regular C corporation.

Form 1120S generally must be filed by March 15th of the year immediately following the calendar year covered by the return or, if a fiscal year (a year ending on the last day of a month other than December) is used, by the 15th day of the third month immediately following the last day of the fiscal year. The corporation must complete a Schedule K-1 for each person who was a shareholder at any time during the tax year and file it with the IRS along with Form 1120S. The second copy of the Schedule K-1 must be mailed to the shareholder.

Visit the IRS "S" corporation Web page to learn more.
http://www.irs.gov/businesses/small/article/0,,id=98263,00 .html

You establish an "S" corporation when you file with the IRS for your FEIN (Federal Employer Identification Number). You simply check the option for "S" corporation on the application.

Advantages:
1. **Paying taxes:** You pay your income taxes when you file annually.

2. **Pass-Through taxation:** (i.e., no double taxation). In other words you do not pay taxes as corporate income then again as personal income earned from the company. Two levels of taxation can often be avoided.
3. **Less Tax:** There is no accumulated earnings tax.
4. **Liability Protection:** There is limited liability protection. It offers the protection of a C corporation. Shareholders and owners are typically not personally responsible for the debts and liabilities of the business.
5. **Administration:** Required to follow the same internal and external corporate formalities, such as adopting bylaws, issuing stock, holding initial and then annual meetings of shareholders and directors, and keeping the minutes from these meetings with the corporate records. Examples of external requirements include filing annual reports, which are required by the state and paying the necessary annual fees.

Disadvantages:
1. **Alternative Minimum Tax (AMT):** Individual alternative minimum tax consequences may arise and force you to pay at a higher tax rate.
2. **Public Offering:** The S Corp. may not be brought forward in a public offering to raise capital.
3. **Limited Shareholders:** Limited to no more than 100 shareholders.
4. **Residency requirement:** Shareholders must be U.S. citizens or residents and must be physical entities (a person).
5. **Administration requirements:** Required to follow the same internal and external corporate formalities, such as adopting bylaws, issuing stock, holding initial and annual meetings of shareholders and directors, and keeping the minutes from these meetings with the corporate records. Examples of external requirements include filing annual reports,

which are required by the state, and paying the
necessary annual fees.

SUBCHAPTER C CORPORATION:
C corporations are ordinary business corporations that have not
elected to be treated as Subchapter S corporations.

A C corporation (or **C corp.**) is a corporation in the United States
that, for federal income tax purposes, is taxed under 26 U.S.C. § 11
and Subchapter C (26 U.S.C. § 301 et seq.) of Chapter 1 of the
Internal Revenue Code.

Visit the IRS C Corporation Web page to learn more.
**http://www.irs.gov/businesses/small/article/0,,id=98240,00
.html**

Advantages:
1. **Limited Liability:** Shareholders and owners are
    typically not personally responsible for the debts and
    liabilities of the business.
2. **Number of Shareholders:** No restriction as to the
    number of shareholders.

3. **Losses carry forward:** Favorable loss carry-forward
    rules. Financial losses experienced in one year can
    be carried forward to future years.
4. **Who can be shareholders:** Shareholders can be
    individuals or other entities (foreign or domestic).
5. **Classes of Stock:** Can have multiple classes of
    stock. Each class of stock can have different voting
    rights.
6. **Going Public (IPO):** C corporations can make
    public offerings and have their stocks traded on a
    stock exchange.

Disadvantages:
1. **Two levels of taxation.** C corporations pay
    corporate income tax and dividends paid out to
    shareholders are taxed as well.

2. **Accumulated income tax:** Must pay corporate income taxes.
3. **Pass-Through losses:** Pass-through of losses to investors is not available.
4. **Administration requirements:** Required to follow the same internal and external corporate formalities, such as adopting bylaws, issuing stock, holding initial and then annual meetings of shareholders and directors, and keeping the minutes from these meetings with the corporate records. Examples of external requirements include filing annual reports, which are required by the state and paying the necessary annual fees.

LIMITED LIABILITY CORPORATION (LLC):

A **limited liability company** is a relatively new form of entity that combines the advantage of a partnership with the advantage of a corporation's limited shareholder liability, even if the owners participate in the management of the company (abbreviated by **L.L.C.** or **LLC**). The owners have limited personal liability for the actions and debts of the company.

An LLC can have one or multiple owners. An "L.L.C" with multiple owners may choose to be treated for **U.S. federal taxation** purposes as a **partnership** or sometimes an **S Corporation** with the benefit of pass-through taxation.

An LLC can elect to be **Member-Managed** or **Manager-Managed**.

A few types of businesses generally cannot be LLCs, such as banks and insurance companies. Check your state's requirements and the federal tax regulations for further information. There are special rules for foreign LLCs.

Members may include individuals, corporations, other LLCs and foreign entities. There is no maximum number of members.

Member-Managed: Choosing to operate by member management creates a flat member or partnership structure.

Choosing manager management creates a two-tiered management structure potentially convertible into a corporation.

Manager-Managed: Managers are the individuals who are responsible for the maintenance, administration and management of the affairs of an LLC. In most states, the managers serve a particular term and report to and serve at the discretion of the members. Specific duties of the managers may be detailed in the articles of organization or the operating agreement of the LLC. In some states, the members of an LLC may also serve as the managers.

Owners: Owners are sometimes referred to as "Members." Unless the articles of organization or operating agreement provide otherwise, each governing person or member has an equal vote in the management of the LLC.

Articles of Organization: LLCs are organized with a document called the "articles of organization," or "the rules of organization" specified publicly by the state; additionally, you will have to file articles of organization with the Secretary of State and pay the required fees. Articles may be prepared by a lawyer or filed by you.

Operating Agreement: The operating agreement is a contract among the members of an LLC and the LLC governing the membership, management, operation and distribution of income of the company. Although it is not required in many states to draft an operating agreement, it is advisable. It's just like corporate by-laws or partnership agreements.

LLC Taxes:

1. Tax forms are complex.

2. As a partnership, the entity's income and deductions attributed to each member are reported on that owner's tax return.

3. LLCs can lose their tax advantage without the partnership structure.

4.   An LLC passively investing in real estate and owned by a single member would have its income and deductions reported directly on the owner's individual tax return on a Schedule E tax form.

5.   And an LLC owned by a corporation--in other words, an LLC with a single corporate member-- would be treated as an incorporated branch and have its income and deductions reported on the corporate tax return, creating double taxation.

6.   For additional information on the kinds of tax returns to file, how to handle employment taxes and possible pitfalls refer to Publication 3402, Tax Issues for Limited Liability Companies (PDF).

7.   To be treated as a corporation, an LLC has to file a Form 8832, Entity Classification Election (PDF) and elect to be taxed as a corporation.

8.   If a Single Member LLC does not elect to be a corporation it will be classified by the IRS as a "Disregarded Entity" which is taxed as a **Sole Proprietor,** for **income tax purposes**.

9.   A multi-member LLC that does not elect will be classified by the IRS as a partnership.

10. If an SMLLC has or intends to have employees, the EIN rules are different. If there is or will be employment tax reporting, both the single member owner and the SMLLC will need an EIN (two EIN's). If the SMLLC has already received an EIN for reasons set out in the above paragraph, then only the owner will need to file the SS-4 and be assigned an EIN.

11. After January 1, 2009, Notice 99-6 is obsolete and the SMLLC will be responsible for collecting, reporting and paying over employment tax obligations using the name and EIN assigned to the LLC.

LLC EIN:

If a SMLLC, whose taxable income and loss will be reported by the single member owner, needs an EIN to open a bank account or if state tax law requires the SMLLC to have a federal EIN, then the

SMLLC can apply for and obtain an EIN. If the SMLLC has no employees, it will not use this EIN for any federal tax reporting purpose.

Learn more about LLC from the IRS LLC Web page.
http://www.irs.gov/businesses/small/article/0,,id=98277,00 .html

Advantages:
1. **Administrative paperwork:** Much less administrative paperwork and record keeping is required than a corporation.
2. **Number of Shareholders:** No restriction on the number or nature of shareholders.
3. **Pass-Through taxation** (i.e., no double taxation)**:** Unless the LLC elects to be taxed as a C corporation. In other words you do not pay taxes as corporate income then again as personal income earned from the company.
4. **Limited Liability:** Means that the owners of the LLC, called "members," are protected from some liability for acts and debts of the LLC, but are still responsible for any debts beyond the fiscal capacity of the entity.
5. **Separate Entities:** LLCs in most states are treated as entities separate from their members, whereas in other jurisdictions case law has developed deciding LLCs are not considered to have separate juridical standing from their members.
6. **Flexible Profit Distribution:** Limited liability companies can select varying forms of distribution of profits. Unlike a common partnership where the split is 50/50, LLCs have much more flexibility.
7. **No Minutes:** Corporations are required to keep formal minutes, have meetings and record resolutions. The LLC business structure requires no

corporate minutes or resolutions and is easier to operate.

Disadvantages:

1. **Franchise Tax:** A handful of states (such as Alabama, California, Kentucky, New York, Pennsylvania, Tennessee and Texas), levy a **franchise tax or capital values tax on LLCs** (Beginning in 2007, Texas has replaced its franchise tax with a "margin tax"). In essence, this **franchise tax** is the "fee" the LLC pays the state for the benefit of limited liability. The franchise tax can be an amount based on revenue, profits, the number of owners, the amount of capital employed in the state, a combination of those factors or simply a flat fee, as in Delaware.

2. **Financing:** It may be more difficult to raise business financing for an LLC as investors may be more comfortable investing funds in the better-understood corporate form with a view toward an eventual IPO. One possible solution may be to form a new corporation and merge into it, dissolving the LLC and converting it into a corporation.

3. **Disregarded Entity:** Some states do not fully treat LLCs in the same manner as corporations for liability purposes. Instead they treat them more as a disregarded entity, meaning an individual operating a business as an LLC may in such a case be treated as operating it as a **sole proprietorship**, or a group operating as an LLC may be treated as a **general partnership.**

4. **Operating Agreement:** Although there is no statutory requirement for an operating agreement in most states, members who operate without one may run into problems.

5. **Corporate Governance:** Unlike corporations, they are not required to have a board of directors or officers.

6. **Title Confusion:** The principals of LLCs use many different titles -- e.g., member, manager,

7. Managing member, managing director, chief executive officer, president and partner. As such, it can be difficult to determine who actually has the authority to enter into a contract on the LLC's behalf.

8. **Foreign Jurisdiction:** Taxing jurisdictions outside the U.S. are likely to treat a U.S. LLC as a corporation, regardless of its treatment for U.S. tax purposes.; for example if a U.S. LLC does business outside the U.S., or a resident of a foreign jurisdiction is a member of a U.S. LLC.

9. **Limited Life:** Corporations can live forever, whereas a LLC is dissolved when a member dies or undergoes bankruptcy.

10. **Going Public:** Business owners with plans to take their company public, or issuing employee shares. In the future, may be best served by choosing a corporate business structure.

11. **Alternative Minimum Tax:** Individual alternative minimum tax consequences may arise.

WHERE TO INCORPORATE

When you decide to form a business you must incorporate or Register the business with a state. However, the state you choose will determine the benefits your business receives. For example, incorporating your business in Delaware or Nevada provides more benefits than any other state. These are the options for incorporation.

- **State Incorporation**
- **Delaware Corporation**
- **Nevada Corporation**

STATE INCORPORATION:

Incorporating in a particular state is done by filing with the respective Secretary of State office. It involves downloading the file from the state's Web site filling it out and mailing it to the business department. In some states this can be done online. Processing can take seven days to several weeks. Expedited service (which comes with an additional fee) can take one to three days. (**See Appendix B** for a list of Web address by state where you can incorporate)

DELAWARE INCORPORATION:

A Delaware Corporation is a corporation chartered in the U.S. state of Delaware. Delaware is well-known as a corporate haven, and thus, over 50% of U.S. publicly-traded corporations and 58% of the Fortune 500 companies are incorporated in the state.

Legal Benefits

Because of the extensive experience of the Delaware courts it has a more well-developed body of case law than other states, which serve to give corporations and their counsel greater guidance on matters of corporate governance and transaction liability issues. Disputes over the internal affairs of Delaware corporations are usually filed in the Delaware Court of Chancery, which is a separate court of equity (as opposed to a court of law). Because it

is a court of equity, there are no juries and its cases are heard by the judges called chancellors. There is currently one Chancellor and four Vice Chancellors. The court is a trial court, with one chancellor hearing each case. Litigants may appeal final decisions of the Court of Chancery to the Delaware Supreme Court.

The status of Delaware as a corporate haven is not recent; following the example of New Jersey, which enacted corporate-friendly laws at the end of the 19th century, Delaware played the game of fiscal competition by adopting in 1899 a general incorporation act aimed at attracting more businesses. More broadly, many U.S. states have usury laws limiting the amount of interest a lender can charge, but federal law allows corporations to "import" these laws from their home state. Delaware (among others) has relatively lax interest laws, in affect allowing banks to charge as much as they want, hence the preponderance of credit card companies and other lenders in the state.

However, other states like Nevada are friendlier to corporations in certain respects, especially in offering protection from hostile takeovers.

Tax Benefits
Some mistakenly believe that Delaware's pre-eminence is related to the fact that it charges no income tax to corporations not operating within the state. However, in this respect Delaware is no different from other states, as no state charges income tax on out-of-state income.

A state does levy a franchise tax on corporations incorporated in it. Franchise taxes in Delaware are actually far higher than in most other states which typically charge little to nothing beyond corporate income taxes on the portion of the corporation's business done in that state. For instance, Nevada does not have a franchise tax. Delaware's franchise taxes supply about one-fifth of its state revenue.

Disadvantages to Delaware Corporations
- Delaware's formation and annual fees are substantially higher than most other jurisdictions.
- The Delaware Division of Corporations charges a fee to tell you the status of an entity. This is unusual as they are de-facto charging a fee to tell you if you actually owe a fee.

Delaware Registered Agents:
http://www.corp.delaware.gov/agents/agts.shtml

Delaware registered agents are personnel that can help you in starting a business or incorporating in Delaware. This registered agent service was founded to serve the entrepreneurs in the process of their business formation.

NEVADA INCORPORATION:

Nevada has changed some of its corporate laws to build a more favorable environment in which corporations can be set up.

Legal Benefits:
- The identities of shareholders do not have to be disclosed in the corporation's public records.
- Directors, officers and shareholders can be non-residents of the state of Nevada.
- One person can hold all corporate offices.
- You do not have to pay state annual franchise tax.
- There are no state corporate taxes on profits.
- You do not have to pay state personal income tax.
- The formation of a corporation in Nevada is easy and quick.
- To setup a corporation in Nevada you must have a legal address and registered agent within the state.

Another advantage for incorporating your business in Nevada is that it has no corporate income tax, along with four other states. In addition, to strict privacy regulations corporations in Nevada can keep their public records secret, giving a business anonymity and confidentiality. Corporations also get liability protection as well as flexibility regarding management in Nevada as the state prohibits information sharing with the IRS.

Registered (Resident) Agents:
http://sos.state.nv.us/business/comm_rec/ralist/

If your business will not reside in the state of Nevada you can use the Registered/Resident Agent to help you setup the business and address the legal requirements for the state of Nevada.

OTHER ENTITIES YOU HAVE TO REGISTER WITH

In addition to registering with the business with the state you may also have to file the incorporation papers with the **county** and **city** in which the business resides. Do a search on the Web to find the office for your county and city.

There is normally a small fee that is required to file with the county and city.

Cities that have a sales tax also require businesses located in the city to register for a **city sales tax ID**.

WHAT IS NORMALLY REQUIRED TO FILE INCORPORATION PAPERS

Business address: This is the address where you actually do business - it cannot be a post office box number.

Mailing address: If you prefer to have your forms and correspondence mailed to an address other than your business address. This address can be a post office box number.

Business organization type: This is based on your federal income tax classification (*e.g.*, corporation, partnership, sole proprietor) and whether your business is a Limited Liability Company (LLC).

Description of the business: What type of goods and/or services will be provided?

Personal information: If an owner, officer, member, manager, shareholder, executor or trustee is an *individual*, you must have their legal name and Social Security number (SSN). If an owner, officer, member, manager, shareholder, executor or trustee is a *business*, you must have the legal name and FEIN.

Responsible party: The name, address and SSN of each person who will be responsible for filing returns and paying the tax due.

Federal Employer Identification Number (FEIN): If you are required to and have obtained your FEIN, please provide your FEIN in your registration or contact us when you receive it.

The number and type of stocks (or Shares) that will be issued:

Common Stock: Common shares represent ownership in a company and a claim (dividends) on a portion of profits.

Dividend is not guaranteed with common stock. Investors get one vote per share to elect the board members who oversee the major decisions made by management. Common stocks entail the most risk; if a company goes bankrupt and liquidates, the common shareholders will not receive money until the creditors, bondholders and preferred shareholders are paid.

Preferred Stock: Preferred stock represents some degree of ownership in a company but it usually doesn't come with the same voting rights. Investors are usually guaranteed a fixed dividend forever with preferred stock. Another advantage is that in the event of liquidation preferred shareholders are paid off before the common shareholder (but still after debt holders). Preferred stock may also be callable, meaning that the company has the option to purchase the shares from shareholders at any time for any reason (usually for a premium).

Different Classes of Stock: Common and preferred are the two main forms of stock. However, it's also possible for companies to customize different classes of stock in any way they want. The most common reason for this is the company wanting the voting power to remain with a certain group; therefore, different classes of shares are given different voting rights. For example, one class of shares would be held by a select group who are given ten votes per share while a second class would be issued to the majority of investors who are given one vote per share. When there is more than one class of stock, the classes are traditionally designated as Class A and Class B.

CORPORATE GOVERNANCE

Bylaws are internal corporate documents that stipulate how the organization is managed.

State laws require the corporations adopt **bylaws,** hold an **annual shareholders meeting**, form a **Board of Directors** and hold an annual **Board of Directors** meeting. State law also requires that the minutes of the meeting be recorded.

There are no requirements to provide a report to the states on whether or not the meetings took place, nor are they required to submit the minutes of the meetings. The minutes of the meeting are internal documents to the corporation.

After you form the organization you need to create and issue stocks to the owners of the organization. The link below will take you to organizations that sell stock certificates and corporate seals. You can purchase the stock certificates and edit them with the appropriate owner information.

Below is a list of some vendors that provide corporate seal and stock certificate kits. *Visit The Small Business Zone Web site (**http://www.sbz1.com**) for a more extensive list.*

2.   Attorneys Corporation Service
http://www.attorneyscorpservice.com/products/corporate-kits.asp
Provides bylaw kits that include bylaws, stock certificates, company seal, etc. **COST: Starts at $55.**

American Notary Supply
http://corporate.americannotarysupply.com/level2.cfm/Sear ch/CatSearch/LevelOne/Corporate
Sells corporate seals. **COST: Starts at $23.99**

Corporate Bylaws Net
http://www.corporate-bylaws.net
An online service that you can subscribe to. **COST: Start at $65.**

BOARD OF DIRECTORS:

The Board of Directors performs the following functions:

- Selects and appoints or removes a CEO
- Provides CEO advice and counsel
- Monitors CEO performance

- Selects and removes other Board Members
- Provides financial expertise
- Contacts to external community
- Enhances firm reputation and credibility
- Provides technological expertise
- Develops management succession plans
- Reviews management proposals
- Assesses its own performance
- Serves as a Court of Appeal in personnel matters

How many Board Members (Directors) can you have?

State laws also determine the minimum and maximum number of individuals you can have on the Board of Directors. Depending on the state this number could range from one to as many as you want. Most states leave it up to the corporation to stipulate the requirements of the board of directors in their bylaws. If you are the sole owner of your organization then you are the only director, unless you decide to add other members to the board. When you add members to the board you must report this to the respective state.

What are the skill and experience that should be required for Board Members:

Board members are selected to bring certain expertise to the oversight process of the board. For example, you may select someone with an information technology background to provide oversight on subject related matters; someone with a finance and accounting background to provide finance and accounting oversight; or someone with a legal background to provide legal oversight, etc.

Age requirement for Board Members:

State laws require that the minimum age for board members be 18.

Type of Board Members:

There are two types of board members (internal or external):

Internal: An internal board member (director) is someone who has ownership in the organization and also serves as a director.

External (or Independent): An external or independent board member (director) is someone who does not have ownership in the organization but is selected to serve on the board. Public corporations have been required by law to have external or independent board members as a means to provide additional checks and balances to the process.

Board Meetings:
The board of directors is required to meet (by state law) at least once every year.

NON-PROFIT ORGANIZATIONS

Non-profit organizations are business organizations that do not operate to make a profit. However, most non-profit businesses are organized into corporations. Most corporations are formed under the corporations' law of a particular state. Every state has provisions for forming non-profit corporations; some permit other forms, such as unincorporated associations, trusts, etc., which may operate as non-profit businesses on slightly (but sometimes importantly) different terms.

Non-profit organizations are exempt from certain taxes. Section 501 of the Internal Revenue code lists several circumstances under which corporations are exempt from these taxes. Section 501(c)(3) -- the famous one -- describes corporations (1) serving charitable, religious, scientific or educational purposes (2) no part of the income of which "inures to the benefit of" anyone.

Tax-exempt non-profit corporations can, and do, operate in all other particulars like any other sort of business. They have bank accounts, own productive assets of all kinds, receive income from sales and other forms of activity (including donations and grants if they are successful at finding that sort of support), make and hold passive investments, employ staff, enter into contracts of all sorts, etc.

There are some specialized tax rules and accounting practices that apply to non-profit corporations. If they are of a certain size, they are required to disclose many details of their operations to the general public and to state regulators and watchdog agencies using

IRS form 990. This form shows any salaries paid to officers or directors and to the five highest-paid employees and contracts if any receive over $50,000 in the tax year (as of 1998). The form also requires the organization to divide its expenses into "functional categories" -- program, administration and fund-raising -- and report the totals for each along with the amounts expended on each program activity.

For more details on tax exempt organizations consult the *IRS Tax Exempt Organizations Manual (Publication 557)* at http://www.irs.gov/publications/p557/ch03.html

OBTAINING YOUR TAX ID (FEIN)

The FEIN is a tax ID issued by the federal government (the IRS) to organizations doing business in the U.S. in order to establish an account for paying taxes.

When is a Federal Tax ID (FEIN) required?
Corporations or LLCs, employers, and in some states, businesses that are also getting a seller's permit, are required to obtain a Federal Tax ID Number (FEIN).

In general, unless you are a partnership, LLC or corporation you do not need a federal tax identification number. You can use your Social Security number

Applying for a FEIN:
http://www.irs.gov/businesses/small/article/0,,id=98347,00.html

OBTAINING STATE SALES TAX ID

A state sales tax ID is required if your organization sells a product.

You must register with the respective state's Department of Revenue if you conduct business in that state, this includes sole proprietors (individual or husband/wife), exempt organizations, or government agencies withholding for employees.

It is recommended that you contact other federal and state agencies and your units of local government (county, municipal, mass transit districts, *etc.*), to learn if you must register your business with them.

Applying for a state sales tax ID can be done in person or by applying online, depending on the state.

Click on the state below (and navigate the states revenue agencies' sites) to see individual state sales tax ID filing policy and forms.

See Appendix C for a link to states' Web sites to see individual state sales tax ID filing policy and forms.

CHAPER 8

MARKETING

Marketing (or advertising) has been referred to as the engine that drives the train. Marketing is about letting others know what goods/services you have to offer. You have to market in order to increase your customer base and grow your business.

You have many options for how you can market (or advertise) your business to the public. What form is best depends on the goods or service(s) you're offering, your budget, who you want to target and how you want to target them. Some forms of advertising are more expensive than others.

It is more expensive to advertise on TV and in magazines than other forms of marketing, but you can reach a wider audience through these mediums.

Marketing can be accomplished in the areas listed below. Examine the choices below and determine which is best for you.

1. PRESS RELEASE
2. RADIO
3. BILLBOARDS
4. PRINT ADVERTISING
   - Brochures/Flyers
   - Newspapers
   - Magazines
   - Business Cards
5. TV
6. PRODUCT PLACEMENT (MOVIES)
7. MOBILE
8. PUBLIC SPACE
9. INTERNET
10. DIRECT MAIL
11. TELEMARKETING
12. ALTERNATIVE MARKETING

13. TRADE SHOWS/CONVENTIONS/EXPOS
14. CHAMBER OF COMMERCE
15. OTHER BUSINESS NETWORKING
OPPORTUNITIES
16. SELF PROMOTION
17. BUSINESS AWARDS
18. GUERRILLA MARKETING
19. SOCIAL NETWORKING
20. THE MARKETING PLAN

PRESS RELEASE

A press release is a message that goes out to journalists, editors of magazines, newspapers, TV show producers, etc. and notifies them of a potential newsworthy story that they may want to talk or write about on their TV shows, magazines, newspapers, etc. Journalists and editors need new stories to write about and as a result you get free publicity for your business. The only cost to you is the fee for the press release. One press release can go out to thousands of journalists, editors and producers.

A well-written release can dramatically increase your sales, expose your company to the masses and greatly enhance the image of your business or products.

The cost of a press release can range from $0 to $350; the larger the group it's released to, the more it will cost.

To see examples and learn how to write press releases go to these locations.
http://www.publicityinsider.com/release.asp
http://www.free-press-release-center.info/fprctips.html

These are some of the many press release submission services that you can choose from. *Visit The Small Business Zone Web site (**http://www.sbz1.com**) to see a more extensive list.*

!PR Distribution services
http://www.exclamationpr.com/distribution.html

Send your press release to as many as 30,000 media and press outlets. **COST: $145**

PRWeb
http://www.prweb.com/service_features.php
Press releases can go directly to consumers and media through Yahoo! News, Google News as well as popular search engines. Your release is also carried in news feeds for targeted industries. **COST: $80 +**

Press Box
http://www.pressbox.co.uk/cgi-bin/links/add.cgi
A public database that provides "primary source" data for publicity services by having its raw data presented to media outlets. **COST: FREE**

RADIO

Radio advertising offers you the opportunity to deliver a simple yet powerful message to a targeted group of consumers that may be interested in your product or service. It is relatively inexpensive compared to other forms of advertisement. You can write and produce the ad yourself with minimal effort. Another option would be to use the ad creation services offered by some radio stations, or other agencies, and then place the ads on those stations that best serve your market.

Radio stations sell time, and they sell access to markets. The price is based on the radio type (AM/FM), the show, demographics and time of day. Price starts at $15.00 for a 15 second ad and go higher depending on the market and programming for your ad.

When you write your ad, make sure it maintains focused and is in tune with your marketing strategy.

To place an ad you can contact the **radio stations individually** and negotiate for rates or you can utilize a radio **ad placement service.**

- Contacting **radio stations individually** involves more work and may not get you the best price.

- Radio **ad placement services** can generate quick feedback, and gets you the best price.

Below are some of the many radio ad placement services you can use. *Visit The Small Business Zone Web site (**http://www.sbz1.com**) to see a more extensive list.*

Bid4spots
http://www.bid4spots.com/AD_Pros_main.aspx
Bidding site where radio stations bid for advertisers' dollars (Reverse Auction).

DMARC (Google AdWords)
http://www.dmarc.net/
Serves as a one-stop-shop for creating and placing Radio ads. It has a demo tool that shows you how the process works and it can develop cost estimates.

RDR (Radio Direct Response)
http://www.radiodirect.com/pages/promotions.asp
Serves as a one-stop-shop for creating and placing radio ads.

BILLBOARDS

Billboard advertising cost starts at $12.50 for indoor and $200 for outdoor. Cost for billboards in prime locations goes for hundreds and thousands of dollars. Cost is based on the size, location and length of time you want to place the ad. Billboard advertising comes in two forms: **outdoor** and **indoor.**

Outdoor billboard:
These are the large signs you see along the highway, or on sides of buildings.

Indoor billboards
This refers to small signs placed in venues such as restaurants, movie theaters, sports clubs, bars, shopping centers, etc.

Billboard advertising is more expensive than many other advertising methods. However, given the fact that thousands of people per day may be exposed to your message, billboards could be a very cost-effective way of getting your message out.

Billboard Ad Creation:
You can have your ad developed by a third party vendor or you can create it yourself (not recommended), then place your ad with a billboard ad placement agency. You may also have the ad placement agency develop your ad and place it with a billboard ad placement agency (recommended). Most ad placement agencies provide this service for an additional fee (some as low as $225).

Billboard Size:
Check out billboard sizes: typical billboards are 14 by 48 feet, 12 by 24 feet (30-sheet) and 5 by 11 feet (8-sheet). The largest sign is the one you most often notice along the freeway, with this sign you get the maximum exposure.

Your Message:
Keep your billboard message brief and eye-catching. It should be big enough for the audience to read it as they are driving by.

Monitor Your Ads:
You should monitor the rotation and placement of your signs. Notify the company immediately if you discover your ads are not being placed as agreed.

Placing Billboard Ads:
You can place billboard ads by using the service of ad placement agencies that can place your ads locally, regional, nationally or internationally.

Below are some outdoor placement agencies. *Visit The Small Business Zone Web site* **(http://www.sbz1.com**) *to see a more extensive list.*

OGGI
http://www.oggi.co.nz/siteauction.html

Nationwide allows you to place bids for billboard ad space.

Billboard Connection
http://www.billboardconnection.com/products/index.asp
Builds and displays your signs on billboards nationwide. (Additional services include: posters, bus shelters, transit bus, bus shelters, mall display, taxi display, mobile billboards, airport displays, sports stadium, transit and subways, etc.)

Global Outdoor Services
http://www.billboards.com/
Builds and displays your signs on billboards nationwide. (Additional services include: posters, bus shelters, transit bus, bus shelters, mall display, taxi display, mobile billboards, airport displays, sports stadium, transit and subways, etc.)

Below are some indoor placement agencies. *Visit The Small Business Zone Web site (**http://www.sbz1.com**) to see a more extensive list.*

Ad Here Media
http://www.adheremedia.com/adh_au.html
Place ads nationwide in restrooms, night clubs, restaurants, bars, sports centers, etc.

Alloy Media Marketing
http://www.alloymarketing.com/media/outofhome/index.html
Place ads nationwide in venues such as schools, colleges, theaters, military, night life, etc.

Creative Indoor Ads
http://www.creativeindoorads.com/

Place ads in venues such as restaurants, bars, sports bars, night clubs, entertainment venues, etc. **COST: $25 - $200** for three

PRINT ADVERTISING

Print advertising includes flyers, brochures, newspaper advertising, magazines and business cards. Among these, magazines are the most expensive form of advertising. See below for more details on each of these methods of print advertising.

Flyers & Brochures:
Flyers and brochures are also a cost effective way to get your message out to potential consumers of your goods or service. Cost for these products start at $99 per 5,000 and goes higher. There are five ways you can approach this method of advertising.

1. You can use programs such as Microsoft PowerPoint, Microsoft Publisher, Adobe Illustrator and other tools to create and distribute your own flyers and brochures.

2. You can use the above tools to create an electronic copy and send them to a printing service that will print and <u>return them to you for distribution</u>.

3. You can create and print them yourself then use the services of organizations that do the distribution.

4. You use the services of organizations that will create, print and send the hard copies to you for distribution.

5. You can also use the services of organizations that will create, print and distribute them for you.

Below are some vendors you can use to get your flyers and brochures developed. *Visit The Small Business Zone Web site (http://www.sbz1.com) to see a more extensive list.*

Overnight Prints
http://www.overnightprints.com
Print and ship your flyers/brochures to you overnight. **COST: $289.95 (10,000 = 4" x 6" single sided)**

Nitro Print
http://www.nitroprint.com/html/
Create and ship flyers/brochures to you within 24 hours. **COST: $170 (10,000)**

Copy World
http://www.copyworldinc.com/
Print and ship your flyers/brochures to you within 24   hours. **COST: $99 (5,000 = 4" x 6" single sided)**

Newspaper Advertising:
There are two ways you can approach newspaper advertising:

1. Most states have a statewide, or regional wide, network that can place your ads for you. Their prices are inexpensive. This option saves you the trouble of having to contact every newspaper in order to place your ads.

2. The second option is to contact every newspaper you want to place the ad with and place your ad with them. This is more time consuming and it tends to cost more.

Below are some statewide or regional networks you can use to place your ads. *Visit The Small Business Zone Web site (**http://www.sbz1.com**) to see a more extensive list.*

New England Newspaper Association
http://www.nenpa.com/adnetworks
Provides one-stop ad placement service for 6 New England states.

Washington Newspaper Publishers Association
http://www.wnpa.com/display_advertising/
Provides a one-stop-shop for the placement of ads in newspapers throughout Washington, the northwest or nationally.

Iowa Newspapers Association
http://www.inanews.com/advertisers/placeanad.php
Provides nationwide ad placement services.

Magazine Advertising:
Magazine advertising does not come cheap. Advertising in
magazines with a large national publication starts in the tens of
thousands of dollars. However, you can find advertising
opportunities at a more inexpensive cost. A commitment for a
certain number of publishing is usually required. There are literally
thousands of magazines that are published in the U.S. Locate the
magazine you wish to advertise in and contact them directly.

*Visit The Small Business Zone Web site (**http://www.sbz1.com**) to see
an extensive list of magazines.*

Business Cards:
Another way to promote your business is with business cards.
Everyone you come in contact with is an opportunity to promote
your business. Business cards can be produced at costs starting at
$39.95 for 1,000 cards.

Below are some business card vendors you can use to place your
ads. *Visit The Small Business Zone Web site (**http://www.sbz1.com**)
to see a more extensive list.*

Overnight Prints
http://www.overnightprints.com
Design your card online and they will print and ship your cards to
you. **COST: $39.95 = 1,000**

Vista Prints
http://www.vistaprint.com/vp/business_cards/plus_letter
ead.aspx?mk=Business
Design your card online and they will print and ship your cards to
you. **COST: $Regular: $3.99 = 250 /Magnetic: $49.99 = 500**

Prints Made Easy
http://www.printsmadeeasy.com/

Design your card online and they will print and ship your cards to you. **COST: $135.99 = 5,000**

TELEVISION

TV advertising is placing commercials (video advertisements) on local or national TV. TV advertising costs start at $300 for a 15 second ad on local TV during non-primetime shows then ascends to over one million dollars for spots on primetime shows on national TV. It is the most expensive form of advertising.

However, it offers the greatest opportunity to reach a wider audience.

To place commercials on national TV you first have to have the commercial made. This can be done one of several ways: you can create it yourself or you can contact an ad agency.

Getting the ad on the air requires taking advantage of the services of an ad agent, ad agency or contacting the TV station directly.

What you should know about Ad Agents/Agencies:

If you use the service of an ad agency, they should only make money when you do. Ad agencies get a 15% "agency discount," or commission, from TV stations where they place your advertising. If you pay your agent $2,000 for TV ads the agent keeps $300 and pays the TV station $1,700.

Watch out for agencies that attempt to overdo commercial production in order to increase profits. Some agencies get the bulk of their income from the production of commercials.

Placing ads on TV is not necessarily a high cost venture. There are opportunities for getting your ads on TV at a very low cost; you have to shop around.

Ad production costs depend on the elements you want to include in the ad.

The cost for running the ad on TV depends on the time slot, programming and market you want to run your ad in.

You should contact multiple agencies and request a quote for free. Go with the one that best suits your needs.

You can also sell your product on TV through a sign out shopping service such as QVC or HSN. It requires that you fill out an online application, wait several weeks for feedback from the product evaluation, schedule a meet with the company representatives to demonstrate your product and it may also involve attending the local "qualify meeting." HSN may require payment to get your product on the air; QVC does not.

Below are some commercial vendors you can use to place your ads. *Visit The Small Business Zone Web site (**http://www.sbz1.com**) to see a more extensive list.*

Spot Runner
http://www.spotrunner.com/
Produce ads and place them on local or national TV with spot runner. **COST: starts at $1,999.**

Google AdWorks
http://www.google.com/adwords/tvads/
Produce your own ad and place it on national TV with Google AdWorks.

Gameshow Placement LTD
http://www.gameshowplacements.com/
"Give" your product away as a prize and receive a 10-second promotional spot on top game and talk shows.

SpotXchange
http://www.spotxchange.com/?GCID=S19007x001
SpotXchange is the Internet's first platform that allows online video publishers to auction off available in-stream video ad slot inventory. Media buyers, advertisers and agencies use SpotXchange's self-service tools to load commercials and target ad slots by region, time of day, publisher and category/content.

PRODUCT PLACEMENT

This is placing the product or service you offer directly into the movies, music videos or TV shows. It becomes part of the scene or the script. It usually costs a fraction of the cost of a regular 30 second TV commercial. Once placed, it is there forever and will continue to be seen in the future during reruns, syndication, etc.

The cost starts at $2,500. However, prices can go in the tens of thousands of dollars. Other methods of payment include providing free products to the production company crews in return for the service, etc.

Below are some product placement vendors you can use to place your ads. *Visit The Small Business Zone Web site* (**http://www.sbz1.com**) *to see a more extensive list.*

Creative Entertainment Services
http://www.acreativegroup.com/ces/
Provides product placement services in movies, music videos and TV shows.

HERO Entertainment
http://www.heropp.com/corporate/behind.php
Provides product placement services.

Game Show Placements
http://www.gameshowplacements.com/
Get free product placement service by giving your product for free as prizes.

MOBILE ADVERTISING

Mobile advertising is advertising space on displays affixed to moving vehicles or positioned in the common areas of transit stations, terminals and airports (includes: transit advertising, mobile billboard displays, bus displays, rail displays, airport displays, aerial displays, taxi displays and auto raps).

Below are some vendors that provide mobile advertising services. *Visit The Small Business Zone Web site (**http://www.sbz1.com**) to see a more extensive list.*

1-800-Great Ad
http://www.1800greatad.com/advertising/mobile-advertising.htm
Provides all forms of mobile outdoor advertising: helium balloons, inflatable products, cool air balloons, sky dancing, aerial banners, mobile billboards, trucks, etc.

National Transit Media
http://www.nationaltransitmedia.com/TransitAdvertising/
Provide ad placement services for all major metropolitan transportation system (buses) across the country.

Gateway Outdoor Advertising
http://www.gatewayoutdoor.com/transit.htm
Provides transit ad placement services at bus stops, on trains and buses for many public transportation systems across the U.S.

Clear Channel Airports
http://www.clearchannelairports.com
Places ads in airports throughout the U.S.

Marketing AD Ventures
http://www.adsoutdoor.com
Place ads on (top) taxis nationwide.

AVIAD
http://www.aviad.com
Provides aerial ad service (such as aerial banner towing, sky writing, and skyboard) nationwide and internationally. The average cost for one hour of flight is $475. The average cost for aerial banner production is $1,200.

PUBLIC SPACE

Public space advertising includes: benches, newsstands, news racks, kiosks, public telephones, shopping mall displays, in-store displays and convenience store displays.

Bench advertising is an effective way to get your message out. It is visible to pedestrians, vehicular traffic and passengers on bus transportation. It is particularly effective for targeting commuters heading to work, school, etc.

Bench ads are usually in the size of 24"H x 84"W panels. However, the size depends on the dimensions of the bench. The cost of bench ads starts at $80 per month, per bench.

Below are some vendors that provide public space advertising

services. *Visit The Small Business Zone Web site* (*http://www.sbz1.com*) *to see a more extensive list.*

Carney Media
http://www.vanwagner.com/
Place ads on outdoor benches nationwide.

CBS Outdoor
http://www.carneym.com/details.html
Place ads on outdoor benches nationwide

Van Wagner
http://www.cbsoutdoor.com/media_item.php?itemId=67
Place ads at outdoor locations such as sporting arenas, shopping centers, etc., nationwide.

INTERNET ADVERTISING

Internet advertising is a relatively cheap way to advertise your business. It's one of the cheapest ways to advertise your business. Costs start at $0 and go into the hundreds of dollars. You can engage in free exchange of links or ads with other Web sites to mutually promote each other's business. You can also purchase ad space on prominent Web sites that have a captive audience who will see your ad.

Forms of Internet Advertising:

Banner Ads:
These are ads that scroll along the top of the screen horizontally.

Pop-ups:
These are ads that pop-up in small windows in front of the current viewing screen.

Pop-under:
These are ads that pop-up in small windows behind the current viewing screen.

Online Classifieds:
Places an ad about your company on another Web site; this type of ad normally appears on the left, right or top of the web page.

Search Engines:
These are services that scan and index the web and make it easy for users surfing the web to find what they are looking for. Examples of search engines include Yahoo, Google, Excite, Alta Vista, Web Crawler, etc.

Qualified Visitors:
These are Web users who are looking for specific products or services. They identify themselves as such by choosing to accept advertisements on specific products or services in return for getting free products or services. For example, a Web user can agree to accept advertisements from a landscaping service in return for getting a free download of a game.

Pay-Per-Click Ads:
These are ads that you placed on a Web site or a search engine, for which you agree to pay the Web site owner or search engine a fee every time someone clicks on your ad.

E-mail:
Send your ad via e-mail to thousands of recipients. There are
services that will enable you to send thousands of e-mails without
them appearing as SPAM mail.

Shopping Portals/Online Malls:
Shopping portals are sites that offer access to online shopping.
They host a community of individually owned shops. The "mall"
owner provides the online store front and the tools for the
individual store owner to setup, manage and maintain their shops.
Examples of this include Yahoo and EBay.

Online Directory:
An electronic directory that is accessible over the Internet. It
allows for businesses to list their company information which can
be searched and accessed worldwide; examples of this include the
online versions of the Yellow Pages, White Pages and People
Finders.

Paid Search:
You can pay a search engine to list your Web site in the top 10
ranking of most requested Web pages.

Sponsored Search:
You pay a fee to have your Web link appear in the right column of
a search page on search engines such as Google and Yahoo.

Web Ranking:
This is the positioning of your Web site in the first 1-5 positions
on the first page in a search engine and keeping it there as the
viewer moves from page to page.

Paid Inclusion:
This is when you pay search engines (Yahoo, Google, etc.) to index
your Web site earlier than it would take to get it done through the
natural process. This means that your Web site would start
showing up in searches earlier.

Insertion Media:
This is the placement of a video ad on a Web page which appears
in a small window as opposed to a static ad.

Redirected Visitors:
Redirects visitors to your site when they try to go to another's whose domain name is no longer in use.

Videos:
Create and place your own videos of your product or service online for the world to see.

Blogging:
Blogs are discussion sites on the Web where people go to discuss and share information about common things of interest. There is a certain trust level among bloggers because people are sharing their personal experiences with an issue or a product. Blogging is a great way to spread information about your business.

Below are some vendors that provide Internet advertising services. *Visit The Small Business Zone Web site (**http://www.sbz1.com**) to see a more extensive list.*

Google AdWorks
https://adwords.google.com/select/Login?sourceid=aso
Promote your ads on Google and through their online advertising network. You determine what you will pay by stipulating your daily and monthly budget. Provides search engine posting, Pay-Per-Click, Paid Inclusion and Web Ranking.

Yahoo
http://sem.smallbusiness.yahoo.com/searchenginemarketing/index.php?cmp=Yahoo&abr=2022403519
Promote your ads on Google and through their online advertising network. You determine what you will pay by stipulating your daily and monthly budget. Provides search engine posting, Pay-Per-Click, Paid Inclusion and Web Ranking.

123 Greetings
http://www.123greetings.com/mediakit/emailad.html
Provides e-mail marketing services. Rent e-mail lists and conduct mass e-mailing.

DIRECT MAIL

Direct mail is the method of mailing a flyer or brochure to prospective customers. It involves obtaining a list of names and addresses of potential customers, creating and printing the flyer or brochure, paying for the postage and processing the documents for the mailing.

There are direct mail companies that provide some or all of the above services for you. There are direct mail companies from

which you can rent or lease a mailing list and do your own mailing. There are also some direct mail companies that rent or lease the mailing list to you and do the mailing for you for a fee. They provide these services through what they call OUTBOUND services.

Companies that provide the mailing service can do this much lower than the normal cost of a stamp because of their special relationship with the post office. For example, they can mail a postcard for as low as $0.16 for postage instead of the current cost of a stamp.

Below are some vendors that provide direct mail services. *Visit The Small Business Zone Web site (**http://www.sbz1.com**) to see a more extensive list.*

Post Card Mania
http://www.postcardmania.com
Provide mailing lists rental service and printing and mailing service.

Direct Mail Services
http://www.directmailsvs.com
Provide mailing lists rental service and printing and mailing service.

Flyerfaucet Printing & Graphics
http://www.flyerfaucet.com
Provide mailing lists rental service and printing and mailing service.

TELEMARKETING

Telemarketing is a form of direct marketing. A salesperson attempts to contact a potential customer directly over the phone and makes a sales pitch. This is also conducted in the form of leaving a recorded message on a potential customer's answering service; this is referred to as outbound telemarketing. Cost for telemarketing services starts in the hundreds range and goes higher.

Below are some vendors that provide telemarketing advertising services. *Visit The Small Business Zone Web site (**http://www.sbz1.com**) to see a more extensive list.*

Rent A Telemarketer
http://www.rentatelemarketer.net
Rent a telemarketer to directly contact potential customers to promote your product or service and create leads.

1-800 Telemarketing
http://www.1800telemarketing.com/
They directly contact potential customers to promote your product or service and create leads.

Telemarketing.com
http://www.telemarketing.com/outbound2.asp
They directly contact potential customers to promote your product or service and create leads.

ALTERNATIVE MARKETING

Alternative marketing includes the following: word of mouth, in theater, helium balloons, inflatable balloons, hot air balloons, beach receptacle cans, phone boots, gas pumps, milk cartoons, restaurants, coffee cups, cup sleeves, milk cartoons, parking lot markers, elevators, pizza boxes, water bottles, medical bands, sidewalk graphics, sporting arenas, theaters, food containers, etc.

The cost for some of these forms of advertising is relatively low. Cost will depend on the quantity and the method you chose to utilize.

Below are some vendors that provide alternative marketing services. Visit The Small Business Zone Web site (**http://www.sbz1.com**) to see a more extensive list.

Branders
http://www.branders.com
Prints your ad on t-shirts and other promotional items such as cups, pens, bags, water bottles, etc.

CafePress
http://t-shirts.cafepress.com
Prints your ad on t-shirts and other promotional items such as cups, pens, bags, bumper stickers, etc.

Cheap Fast Promos
http://cheapfastpromos.com
Promotional items include t-shirts, cups, pens, office products, etc.

TRADESHOWS AND CONVENTIONS

Tradeshows, conventions (or expos) are also events that you can take advantage of to market your business. Every industry has a trade show or convention. Find the one that has the target audience you want to promote your business to. This form of marketing can be expensive. There is normally a cost associated with leasing a space for your booth; this can range from $2,500 to $5,000. You also have to get your display made. The cost for this can range from $1,000 to $3,000.

Below are some vendors that provide tradeshow marketing services. *Visit The Small Business Zone Web site (**http://www.sbz1.com**) to see a more extensive list.*

All Conferences
http://www.allconferences.com
A directory of conferences worldwide.

Biz Tradeshows
http://www.biztradeshows.com
Find trade shows by country and location.

EventsEye
http://www.eventseye.com
Find tradeshows by name, location, date or organizer.   Also allows you search by keyword.

CHAMBER OF COMMERCE

Chamber of Commerce offices can be found nationwide. They are a non-government organization. The chamber consists of businesses of all sizes and industries, as well as non-profit and government organizations. Membership in the local Chamber of Commerce has several benefits:

- It provides an opportunity to market your business as well as offering you the opportunity to meet and network with other business leaders.
- You can also display your marketing brochure at their offices for free.
- They give you access to their member directory so that you can promote your business to their members directly.
- Through their monthly sponsored events you get the opportunity to promote your business.
- The Chamber of Commerce represents your business interest in the legislative process locally and nationally.
- You can learn about your industry by attending industry   specific seminars.

Membership dues in the local Chamber of Commerce is based on the number of employees in your organization. For example, the average dues are:

- 1-5 employees the annual dues is $405.
- 100 employees the annual dues is $1,290.

Investments are deductible from federal and state income tax returns as ordinary and necessary business expenses, not as charitable contributions.

Find local Chamber of Commerce in your area
http://www.uschamber.com/chambers/directory/default.ht
m?n=bd

OTHER BUSINESS NETWORKING OPPORTUNITIES

There are other business networking opportunities across the country that are held in the form of business breakfasts, evening socials, all day events, etc. These events are held locally and nationally by organizations that are formed with the sole interest of offering businesses the opportunity to promote themselves and find new customers. Some organizations require you pay a fee and become a member while others do not require membership but require you to pay for your meals during the events. Some organizations do not take in more than one business in the same industry. This is done to prevent two businesses from competing for the same potential customers.

Business networking organizations across the country manage their meetings differently. Some just provide the opportunity to meet and talk with whomever you choose, while others give you the opportunity to have short meetings with everyone in attendance through two minute round-robin sessions.

Below are some other business networking services. *Visit The Small Business Zone Web site (**http://www.sbz1.com**) to see a more extensive list.*

American Business Women's Association
http://www.abwa.org

A networking organization for women that hold events throughout the country.

Business Networking International
http://www.bni.com/default.aspx?DN=2,1,Documents
An international business networking organization that provides networking opportunities worldwide.

Fast Pitch
http://www.fastpitchnetworking.com
Hold online business networking events as well as face-to-face events throughout the country.

BUSINESS AWARDS

Another way to promote your business is through business award events. By applying for and winning awards your business gains publicity and gets mentioned in places such as industry magazines, Web sites, newspapers and possibly on TV shows.

It costs nothing to apply for these awards. The only requirement is to meet the deadline and requirements for each specific type of award you are applying for.

Below are some other business awards sponsors. *Visit The Small Business Zone Web site (**http://www.sbz1.com**) to see a more extensive list.*

Diversity Business Award
http://www.diversitybusiness.com/businessawards

The American Business Awards (The Stevie)
http://www.stevieawards.com/aba/

The Blue Chip Business Award
http://admin.bluechipaward.com/

GUERRILLA MARKETING

Guerrilla marketing is a term used to describe unconventional marketing tactics, particularly those of low-cost or no-cost. It involves taking some traditional advertising methods and applying them in an unconventional way.

For example, giving out your business cards to potential clients at a social or business gathering is a traditional way of letting others know about your business. Now take the same business card and attach a discount coupon or a dollar bill to it and have some of your friends stand at the street corners in a busy downtown area during rush hour and hand them out to people. Below are some guerrilla marketing methods.

Guerrilla Marketing Ideas:

POST STICKERS: You can place stickers with your logo and other information about your business on areas around town in places such as newspaper stands, light poles, garbage cans, parking meters, etc.

CONTEST ON A STREET CORNER: Put a number on the back of your business card and hand them out to people. Then have someone randomly pick a number. If anyone in the crowd has that number, they become the winner.

BOOKMARKS: Create bookmarks with your business logo and Web site URL and give them away for free.

RELEASE A FREE BOOK: Write a book about the subject area of your business and offer it for free. Put information in the book that would lead readers back to your Web site or your business.

LOCAL MEDIA (THE STUNT): Either pull a stunt, run a promotion or even have one of those warm success stories ("Local man makes it big on the net). You could have people picket your storefront with signs that read "this business is too nice" or "company X" is too good at their job..

BUMPER STICKERS: Create and give out bumper stickers to anyone who will put it on their vehicle. Millions of people will see your advertisement. Think about how much time you spend in rush hour traffic during the week.

SPECIAL VENUES/EVENTS: Special events offer a unique opportunity for lots of people to be looking at your ad. Think of an ad on the back of a t-shirt of someone walking through crowds of thousands. Think of special events such as October Fest, music festivals, art festivals, food festivals, etc. Give the t-shirt away at the event for free, on the condition that they put it on right then and there.

LET'S GO TO THE MALL: The mall also offers us another opportunity to get lots of people looking at the ad on the back of a t-shirt. Take advantage of it. Give out some free t-shirts on the condition that they wear it right then and there.

DONATIONS: Donate your product or service to venues where they can be offered as prizes or rewards. For example, for an organization's Employee-of-the-Month offer an organization the opportunity to give the Employee-of-the-Month winner your service or product for free as part of their winning package. That will be much more appreciated than just a plaque on the wall.

CHARITY: Donate some of the profits you generate every month to charity. Advertise to the public that this is what you're doing. Notify the media to put the word out. The media loves to support a good cause, hence, free publicity. People feel like they're doing something good by helping out the charity by purchasing from you.

Below are some guerrilla marketing service providers. *Visit The Small Business Zone Web site (**http://www.sbz1.com**) to see a more extensive list.*

Alt Terrain
http://www.altterrain.com
Provides guerrilla marketing services such as, street teams, buzz marketing, grassroots marketing, social advertising and postings, etc.

FUSE
http://www.fusemarketing.com
Provides guerrilla marketing services such as, street teams, brand ambassador, flyer distribution, etc.

Elite Marketing Group
http://www.elitemg.com/elite/what_we_do.html
Provides guerrilla marketing services such as street teams, College postings, product demonstration, etc.

SOCIAL NETWORKING

Social networking marketing refers to the use of social networking media to promote your business. Social media encompasses many Internet-based tools that make it easier for people to listen, interact, engage and collaborate with each other. These tools allow you to promote your business by building communities based on common interest, share videos and share your experiences.

Three good reasons why small businesses should take advantage of Social Networking:

1. Social Networking Marketing is a cost effective way for Small Businesses to spread the word about their business. 99% of these resources are free.

2. Reach a diverse and large audience with your message.

3. Get feedback. Learn what consumers and prospects think about your product or service.

Social networking sites includes: Facebook, Twitter, Youtube, Linkedin, MySpace, Ryze, Groupon, Living Social, etc. Let's examine Facebook and Twitter.

Facebook:

Facebook is a social networking site. It is an online community whereby you can communicate and exchange information with other people (called friends). Users can be categorized into groups such as common-interest user groups, workplace, school, college, etc. It allows you to post content by text or video. It requires that users be 13 years or older to sign up for an account. All users must sign up for an account. Membership is free. Facebook allows you to have no more than 5,000 friends.

Facebook was launched in 2004. As of July 2011 Facebook has over 800 million users. It is most popular in English speaking countries such as the U.S., Canada, and the UK. It is also popular in the Middle East, Africa, Latin America, Europe and Asia.

Facebook generates an average of 770 billion page views per month and the average user has over 130 friends. The average user visits the site 40 times per month.

When it comes to using Facebook as a marketing tool for your business you have two choices. You can chose to perform this function "in-house" by yourself or a member of your staff or you can "outsource" it to a different organization that specialize in this function.

Another way to market on Facebook is to use paid advertising. Facebook advertising allow you to create your own ad or get help from the staff. You can also determine your daily spending limits, pick your target audience, demographics and area of interest.

The fees are based on a Cost per Click (CPC) or Cost per one thousand impression (CPM) basis. You get to set your monthly budget and your daily spending limits. You determine what the price per click at the time you place the ad. This is based on the price levels being set by the bidding process. You set your price based on the bidding range. There is a minimum of $0.01 per CPC and $0.02 per CPM.

Learn about the specifics of using Facebook as a marketing tool and using the right Facebook strategy by going to *http://www.sbz1.com* (under Marketing\social networking\Facebook)

Twitter:
Twitter is a tool for "micro-blogging" or posting very short updates, comments or thoughts. Each update is limited to 140 characters. It is an open forum, but you restrict it to the people with which you wish to connect with. It is a text only medium.

Twitter officially launched in 2006 and started growing in 2009. In 2007 the average number of tweets per day was 5,000. In 2011 the average number of tweets per day was 200 million. One billion tweets are now sent every week. An average of 460,000 tweeter accounts are created every day

When it comes to using twitter as a marketing tool for your business you have two choices. You can chose to perform this function "in-house" by yourself or a member of your staff or you can "outsource" it to a different organization that specialize in this function.

Learn about the specifics of using Facebook as a marketing tool and using the right Facebook strategy by going *to* *http://www.sbz1.com* (under Marketing\social networking\Twitter)

Learn about the specifics social networking and how you can take advantage of them to promote your business inexpensively by going to **http://www.sbz1.com** (under Marketing\social networking).

THE MARKETING PLAN

When it comes to writing a marketing plan you have several options.

> 1. You can look at the free **PLAN TEMPLATE** and write your own plan using programs like Microsoft Word.
> 2. You can download **SOFTWARE** that come with templates and use them to write your marketing plan.
> 3. You can use the **PLAN WRITING SERVICES** offered by companies.

Below are some marketing plan tools. *Visit The Small Business Zone Web site (**http://www.sbz1.com**) to see a more extensive list.*

Know This
http://www.knowthis.com/tutorials/principles-of-marketing/how-to-write-a-marketing-plan.htm
Provides a template for writing a marketing plan.

Palo Alto Software[Marketing Plan Pro]
http://www.paloalto.com/marketing_plan_software/?CFID =7548097
Provides software that can be used to create marketing plans. COST: $179.95

Marketing Plan Builder
http://www.marketingplanbuilder.com
Provides software for writing a marketing plan. **COST: Start at $19.95**

CHAPTER 9

HUMAN RESOURCE

Human Resources is the function of managing all aspects of employee affairs. It involves managing the hiring and firing of employees, managing the payroll to ensure employees get paid what they are entitled to and on time, managing employee benefits (such as leave, health benefits and retirement). In addition to managing other aspects of having employees such as ensuring that federal and states laws are being complied with, workplace safety and managing workers compensation.

Good Human Resource management is a good way to avoid legal troubles. Learn more about each aspect of Human Resources below.

HIRING EMPLOYEES

Federal requirements for hiring employees can be found at: http://www.dol.gov/dol/topic/hiring/index.htm
Issues addressed include hiring youth, affirmative action, foreign labor, veterans, workers under 18, drug-free workplace.

Who is an employee:
According to the IRS, "a general rule is that anyone who performs services for you is your employee if you can control what will be done and how it will be done. This is so even when you give the employee freedom of action. What matters is that you have the right to control the details of how the services are performed."[1]

Full Time Employee:
There is no specific number of hours that an employee must work before he becomes a full-time employee under federal law. That definition is created by the employer. Most employers define full-time employees as those who regularly work 35 to 40 hours a week. These employees typically are entitled to benefits such as paid sick leave, vacation and insurance coverage.

Part-Time Employee:
Part-time employees are any employees who work less than a full-time schedule and may receive some benefits.

Independent Contractor:
According to the IRS "a general rule is that you, the payer, have the ***right to control or direct only the result of the work*** done by an independent contractor, and ***not the means and methods of accomplishing the result.***"[2]

BACKGROUND INVESTIGATIONS:
Regardless of the size of your business, pre-employment screening is a necessary hiring practice to avoid lawsuits and costly hiring mistakes. Pre-employment checks include psychological testing, background checks and drug testing to determine the background and identity of the person you are hiring. Over 96% of all employers use background checks.

Before beginning a background check, it's important that your small business complies with governing laws such as the Employee Polygraph Test Protection Act, the Fair Credit Reporting Act and the Americans with Disabilities Act. Consult with local regulators and legal counsel before going too deep into the criminal past of a new hire.

Background checks can access a full range of data including:
- Credit records
- Academic records
- Social security number
- Personal references
- Driving records
- Criminal records
- Workers' compensation
- Certification & License
- Education records
- Past illegal drug use
- Employment history

Below are some background investigation service providers. *Visit The Small Business Zone Web site (**http://www.sbz1.com**) to see a more extensive list.*

Intelius
http://www.intelius.com/search-name.php?ReportType=1
Provides background checks that verify criminal records to credit history. Reports are generated instantly online. **COST: $49.95**

Public Records Now
http://web.public-records-now.com
Provides background checks that verify criminal history to employment history. **COST: Starts at $27.95**

Sentry Link
https://www.sentrylink.com/web/loadCriminalReport.do?
WT.srch=1
Conducts background checks that range from driver's   license to criminal record. **COST: Starts at $19.95**

LEASING EMPLOYEES:
Employee leasing is similar to the process of hiring temporary workers, but the key difference is permanency. A company wishing to pursue employee leasing will first contact a **Professional Employment Organization** (PEO) to discuss its particular employment needs. The PEO or other employment leasing company might set up an interview process for recruiting new staff, or might take responsibility for existing workers. The company can still participate in the hiring process, but any hired personnel will officially work for the employee leasing company. Wages and performance reviews are under the auspices of the employee leasing organization, not the original companies'. Workers are not considered employees of the company in a legal sense, personal injuries and workers' compensation claims become the responsibility of the employee leasing agency. More specifically, a PEO establishes a contractual relationship with its clients whereby the PEO:

- pays wages and employment taxes of the employee out of its own accounts,

- reports, collects, and deposits employment taxes with state and federal authorities,
- establishes and maintains a co-employment relationship with its employees which is intended to be long term and not temporary,
- assumes responsibility as an employer for specified purposes of the workers assigned to the client locations, and
- shares the responsibility of co-employees' wages and safety with the client.

Below are some employee leasing organization service providers. *Visit The Small Business Zone Web site (**http://www.sbz1.com**) to see a more extensive list.*

PEO Employee Leasing
http://peo.alloptions.com/index.asp?id=10561

HR Research Center
http://www.hrresearchcenter.com/peo-overview.jsp?id=1175783259249003027

People Lease
http://www.peoplelease.com

FIRING EMPLOYEES

1. **You should consider firing the employee only if you've done the following:**

a. Given the employee clear indication of what you originally expected from him or her (via a written job description previously provided to him or her).

b. Provided clearly written personnel policies which specify conditions and directions about firing employees, and have the employee initialized a copy of the policy handbook to verify that

he or she had read the policies.

c. Counsel the employee in successive and dated memos

which clearly describe their degrading performance over a specified time despite your specific and recorded offers of assistance and any training provided to the employee.

    d. Clearly observe the employee still having the performance problem after counseling and training.

Note: If the employee is being fired within a probationary period specified in your personnel policies, you may not have to meet all of the above conditions.

2. **Take a day or more to consider what you are about to do.**
3. **If you still decide to fire the employee do so promptly.**
4. **Write a letter of termination to the employee.**
5. **Tell the computer system administrator to change the employee's password(s).**
6. **Meet with the employee, provide them the letter and explain how the termination will occur.**
7. **As with other meetings, make notes of what was said and exchanged.**

Legal risk to firing employees:
You face a significant legal risk every time you fire someone. To avoid lawsuits you should consult an attorney before you take any action against that employee.

Someone who decides to pursue "justice" through the courts will generally claim discrimination. Women, anyone over the age of forty, physically challenged persons, minorities, homosexuals and many other groups are protected by law from discrimination. Courts, especially juries, tend to be highly sympathetic towards fired employees.

Another potential problem you should be aware of is how you handle reference calls for a former, or fired, employee. If you give out any information on such an employee, other than dates of employment and a salary confirmation, you risk a lawsuit.

PAYROLL MANAGEMENT

As your business grows you will begin to hire employees. When you do, it's important that you become familiar with the payroll tax requirements at the state and federal levels. You have to pay employees a salary, withhold payroll taxes, file payroll reports and pay payroll taxes at the state and federal levels. You can do this in-house utilizing payroll software or you can outsource the function to an organization that specializes in providing outsourced payroll solutions.

Below are some payroll management service providers. *Visit The Small Business Zone Web site* (**http://www.sbz1.com**) *to see a more extensive list.*

Intuit Payroll
http://payroll.intuit.com
Paychecks or direct deposit, payroll tax filing, government reporting, direct deposit, federal and state forms etc., payroll reports, deductions, etc.

Advantage Payroll Services, Inc.
http://www.advantagepayroll.com/instant_payroll/instantpayroll.asp
Paychecks or direct deposit, payroll tax filing, government reporting, federal forms, deductions, payroll reports, etc.

CSI Payroll Services
http://www.csipayroll.com
Paychecks or direct deposit, payroll tax filing, government reporting, direct deposit, federal forms, payroll reports, etc.

MANAGING BENEFITS

WAGES:

Fair Labor Standards Act (FLSA):

http://www.dol.gov/compliance/laws/comp-
flsa.htm#related_topics.

"The Fair Labor Standards Act (FLSA) , which prescribes
standards for the basic minimum wage and overtime pay, affects
most private and public employment. It requires employers to pay
covered employees who are not otherwise exempt at least the
federal minimum wage and overtime pay of 1½ times the regular
rate of pay. For nonagricultural operations, it restricts the hours
that children under the age of 16 can work and forbids the
employment of children under the age of 18 in certain jobs deemed
too dangerous. For agricultural operations it prohibits the
employment of children under the age of 16 during school hours
and in certain jobs deemed too dangerous."

Federal Minimum Wage Standards:
"Effective July 24, 2008 the federal minimum wage is not less than
$6.55 per hour. Beginning July 24, 2009 the federal minimum
wage will be $7.25."4

Overtime Pay:
"At least 1½ times an employee's regular rate of pay for all hours
worked over 40 in a workweek."5

Youth Employment:
"An employee must be at least 16 years old to work in most non-
farm jobs and at least 18 to work in non-farm jobs declared
hazardous by the Secretary of Labor. Youths 14 and 15 years old
may work outside school hours in various non-manufacturing,
non-mining, non-hazardous jobs under the following conditions:

No more than
- 3 hours on a school day or 18 hours in a school week;
- 8 hours on a non-school day or 40 hours in a non-
school week.

- Also, work may not begin before 7 a.m. or end after 7 p.m., except from June 1 through Labor Day, when evening hours are extended to 9 p.m. Different rules apply in agricultural employment."[6]

States Minimum Wage:
See states' minimum wages at the URL below.
http://www.dol.gov/esa/minwage/america.htm

States Pay Day:
States require that employees be paid on a weekly, bi-weekly, semi-monthly or monthly basis. To see the individual states' requirements, go to the URL below.
http://www.dol.gov/whd/state/payday.htm

Minimum Paid Rest Period:
States require that employees be given a certain amount of time for each hour of work as paid rest period (for example, 10 minute for every four hours worked). To see the individual states' requirements, go to the URL below.
http://www.dol.gov/whd/state/rest.htm

HEALTH:

Federal law does not mandate employers provide health care for their employees.

Small group health insurance provided by insurers is regulated by the states. All states (except for HI) do not mandate employers provide health care for their employees. However, some states do mandate that certain types of insurance coverage must be provided if employers chose to provide health insurance to their employees

LEAVE:

Under the **Family and Medical Leave Act (FMLA),** "covered employers must grant an eligible employee up to a total of 12 workweeks of unpaid leave during any 12-month period for one or more of the following reasons:

- for the birth and care of the newborn child of the employee,

- for placement with the employee of a son or daughter for adoption or foster care,

- to care for an immediate family member (spouse, child, or parent) with a serious health condition, **or**

- to take medical leave when the employee is unable to work because of a serious health condition."[7]

Vacation:

"The **Fair Labor Standards Act (FLSA)** does not require payment for time not worked, such as vacations, sick leave or federal or other holidays. These benefits are matters of agreement between an employer and an employee (or the employee's representative)."[8]

Sick Leave:

Currently, there are no federal legal requirements for paid sick leave. This matter is usually an agreement between the employee and the employer.

Holidays:

Currently, there are no federal legal requirements for paid holidays. This matter is usually an agreement between the employee and the employer.

RETIREMENT:

Employers can voluntarily establish retirement plans for their employees. When an employer establishes such plan they must comply with the **Employee Retirement Income Security Act of 1974 (ERISA)** located at the following URL:
http://www.dol.gov/dol/topic/health-plans/erisa.htm

Visit the IRS Web site to learn more about setting up retirement plans for small businesses.
http://www.irs.gov/retirement/content/0,,id=97203,00.html

PAYROLL TAXES

In the United States' income tax system, employers are required to withhold a portion of each employee's income and pay it directly to the U.S. Internal Revenue Service. **This Withholding acts as a prepayment of tax they will owe at the end of the year, as well as a direct payment of certain other taxes.**

Withholding, in general, usually refers to a deduction of money from an employee's wages or salary by an employer, for projected or actual income tax liabilities. Taxes that have to be withheld include Social Security and Medicare (also known as FICA).

Social Security:
Social security taxes must be withheld from your employees' wages. **As an employer, you must also pay a matching amount of FICA taxes for your employees. As of 2007, the social security tax rate is 6.2%. The employee must have 6.2% withheld from their wages for social security taxes and the employer pays a matching amount in social security taxes until the employee reaches the wage base for the year.**
The wage base for social security tax $97,500. Once that amount is earned, neither the employee nor the employer owes any social security tax.

Medicare Tax:
The Medicare tax rate is 2.9% for the employee and the employer. The employer must withhold 1.45% of an employee's wages and pay a matching amount for Medicare tax. Unlike the Social Security tax, there is no maximum wage base for the Medicare portion of the FICA tax. Both the employer and the employee continue to pay Medicare tax, no matter how much is earned.

IRS Form W-4:
Have each new employee completes the IRS form W-4. You will use this form to calculate the amount of federal income tax to withhold from the employee's wages. Most of the states have income tax structures that are based on the federal system, so you will use the W-4 to calculate the amount of state income tax to withhold as well.

The amount of a person's federal income tax withholding depends on several factors such as:
- the taxpayer's marital status
- the number of children or dependents the taxpayer has
- whether or not he is an employee IRC 3401
- if the taxpayer wants to claim child tax credits
- if the taxpayer holds two or more jobs
- if the taxpayer plans to itemize
- any tax exemptions from withholding that the taxpayer wants to claim
- any additional amount the taxpayer wants to withhold

Sample Income Tax Calculation:

- $40,000 (adjusted gross income)
- $7,550 × 0.10 = $755
- ($30,650 - $7,550) × 0.15 = $3,465
- ($40,000 - $30,650) × 0.25 = $2,337.50
- Total income tax = $6,557.50 (16.39% of income)

Sample FICA TAX Calculation:

- $40,000 (adjusted gross income)

- $40,000 × 0.062 = $2,480 (Social Security portion)
- $40,000 × 0.0145 = $580 (Medicare portion)
- Total FICA tax = $3,060 (7.65% of income)
. Total federal tax of individual = $9,617.50 (24.04% of income)

(an equal amount of FICA tax must be paid by the employer)

Learn more about payroll tax withholding at the IRS Web site:
http://www.irs.gov/publications/p505/index.html

Follow the IRS guide to learn how to pay payroll taxes:
**http://www.irs.gov/businesses/small/article/0,,id=98818,00
.html**

MANAGING EMPLOYEES

If you are going to manage employees these are some federal guidelines that you should be knowledgeable of:

- Equal Employment Opportunity (EEO)
- ADA (Americans with Disabilities Act)
- ADEA (Age Discrimination in Employment Act)
- Ethnic/National Origin, Color, Race, Religion & Sex Discrimination
- Federal Financial Assistance Programs
- Veterans
- Immigration
- Equal Pay

You can find more details on those areas at the Department of Labor (DOL) Web site:
http://www.dol.gov/dol/topic/discrimination/index.htm
or at **http://www.sbz1.com**

WORKPLACE SAFETY

Maintaining workplace safety is vital to the successful operation of any business. An unsafe workplace is an invitation to lawsuits. This could adversely impact the bottom line; hence, you must be intimately familiar with and enforce the state and federal requirements for maintaining a safe workplace.

Learn more about the federal workplace safety requirements by visiting:
http://www.osha.gov/dcsp/smallbusiness/index.html

Learn more about states' OSHA requirements by visiting OSHA Web site: **http://www.osha.gov/dcsp/osp/faq.html**

Learn about federal workplace poster requirements at the DOL Web site:
http://www.dol.gov/dol/topic/youthlabor/Postingrequirements.htm
See Appendix D for a list of states' sites for safety poster requirements.

WORKERS COMPENSATION

Workers' compensation consists of insurance that pays for medical care and physical rehabilitation of injured workers and helps to replace lost wages while they are unable to work. State laws, which vary significantly, govern the amount of benefits paid and other compensation provisions.

States' laws, (except Texas) requires all business owners to obtain and maintain workers' compensation coverage, especially those with one or more employees. There are very few exceptions to this requirement.

Business owners failing to comply with this law face fines up to $10,000, and may have their business ordered closed until the insurance has been obtained; they will also be held financially

responsible for all costs associated with an employee who sustains a work related injury when the employer has no workers compensation insurance.

Some states require employers obtain workers' compensation insurance from a state license workers compensation insurance provider while others allow for the use of private insurance companies.

If qualified, an employer **may be self-insured** through an approval process overseen by the respective state. For smaller businesses interested in becoming self-insured, there are **associations of self-insured employers** which are groups of employers (generally in the same type of business) which are members of the association.

Visit The Small Business Zone Web site at **www.sbz1.com** *to see a list of states sites for Workers Compensation requirements.*

CHAPTER 10

TAXES

A business is required to pay federal and state corporate taxes. How business taxes are paid depends on the type of organization where the organization is located. A foreign corporation would have a less tax burden than a domestic corporation. Corporate tax rate differ among states. States such as Wyoming, Washington, South Dakota and Nevada have no corporate tax.

Corporations are also required to pay unemployment insurance tax and payroll taxes.

All tax rates are current as the published date of this book and is subject to change.

FEDERAL CORPORATE TAXES

C Corporation:
Most large corporations are classified as C corporations and are required to file a federal corporate income tax return with the IRS every year. The federal corporate tax rate for this type of organization is as follows:

Corporate Tax Rates

Taxable income	Tax rate
First $50,000	15%
$50,001–$75,000	25%
$75,001–$100,000	34%
$100,001–$335,000	39%
$335,001–$10,000,000	34%
$10,000,001–$15,000,000	35%
$15,000,001–$18,333,333	38%
Over $18,333,333	35%

Other types of Organization:
Other types of organization which most small business fall into

(such as S Corp., Sole Proprietor, LLC, etc.) file pay corporate income taxes based on their personal income tax brackets. The personal income tax brackets are as follows:

Taxable income	Tax rate	Your Tax
0 - 8,375	10%	$0.0
8,375 - 34,000	15%	$837.50
34,000 - 82,400	25%	$4,681.25
82,400 - 171,850	28%	$16,781.25
171,850 - 373,650	33%	$41,827.25
373,650 - above	35%	$108,421.25

If you are Married and Filing Jointly and as a Surviving Spouses, your tax rate will be as follows:

Income	Tax Rate	Tax
$0 - $16,750	10%	$0.0
$16,750 - $68,000	15%	$1,675.00
$68,000 - $137,300	25%	$9,362.50
$137,300 - $209,250	28%	$26,687.50
$209,250 - $373,650	33%	$46,833.50
$373,650 & above	35%	$101,085.50

If you are married and filing separately your tax rate will be as follows:

Income	Tax Rate	Tax
$0 - $8,375	10%	$0.0
$11,950 - $45,550	15%	$1,195.00
$45,550 - $117,650	25%	$6,235.00
$117,650 - $190,550	28%	$24,260.00
$190,550 - $373,650	33%	$44,672.00
$373,650 & above	35%	$105,095.00

Personal Services Corporation:
Personal services include any activity performed in the fields of accounting, actuarial science, architecture, consulting, engineering, health (including veterinary services), law and the performing arts.

Personal service corporations are subject to a **flat tax of 35%** regardless of their income.

Personal Holding Company:
A holding company is a company that owns part, all, or a majority of other companies' outstanding stock. It does not produce goods or services it-self instead its only purpose is to own shares of other companies.

Personal holding companies are subject to an additional **15% tax** on any undistributed personal holding company income.

Accumulated Earnings Tax:
In addition to the regular tax, a corporation may be liable for an **additional tax of 15%** on accumulated taxable income in excess of $250,000 ($150,000 for personal service corporations; Code Sec. 531).

STATE CORPORATE TAXES

See **Appendix E** for state corporate tax rates.

UNEMPLOYMENT INSURANCE TAX

Unemployment Insurance (UI) is a federal-state program jointly financed through federal and state employer payroll taxes (federal/state UI tax). Generally, employers must pay both state and federal unemployment taxes if: (1) they pay wages to employees totaling $1,500, or more, in any quarter of a calendar year or (2) they had at least one employee during any day of a week during 20 weeks in a calendar year, regardless of whether or not the weeks were consecutive. However, some state laws differ from the federal law and employers should contact their state workforce agencies to learn the exact requirements.

Federal Unemployment Tax Act (FUTA):
The Federal Unemployment Tax Act (FUTA) authorizes the Internal Revenue Service to collect a federal employer tax used to fund state workforce agencies. Employers pay this tax annually by

filing IRS Form 940. FUTA covers the costs of administering the UI and job service programs in all states. In addition, FUTA pays one-half of the cost of extended unemployment benefits (during periods of high unemployment) and provides for a fund from which states may borrow, if necessary, to pay benefits.

Federal Unemployment Insurance Tax Rate (FUTA):
The FUTA (Federal Unemployment Tax) tax rate is 6.2% of taxable wages. The taxable wage base is the first $7,000 paid in wages to each employee during a calendar year. Employers who pay the state unemployment tax, on a timely basis, will receive an offset credit of up to 5.4% regardless of the rate of tax they pay the state. Therefore, the net federal tax rate is generally 0.8% (6.2% - 5.4%). This would equate to a maximum of $56.00 per employee, per year (.008 X $7,000. = $56.00) in federal tax. State tax rates are based on requirements of individual State law. A table of current tax rates and taxable wage base information for individual states is available in this Web site under "On This Page" Tax Statistics 2002.

State Unemployment Tax Act (SUTA):
The SUTA (State Unemployment Tax Act) paid to state workforce agencies, is used solely for the payment of benefits to eligible unemployed workers.

Domestic Employers Coverage:
Employers of domestic employees must pay state and federal unemployment taxes if they pay cash wages to household workers totaling $1,000, or more, in any calendar quarter of the current or preceding year. A household worker is an employee who performs domestic services in a private home. Examples of household employees are babysitters, caretakers, cleaning people, drivers, nannies, health aides, yard workers and private nurses.

Employers of Agricultural Employees:
Employers must pay federal unemployment taxes if: (1) they pay cash wages to employees of $20,000, or more, in any calendar quarter or (2) in each of the 20 different calendar weeks in the current or preceding calendar year, there was at least one day in which they had 10 or more employees performing service in agricultural labor. The 20 weeks do not have to be consecutive

weeks, nor must they

be the same 10 employees, nor must all employees be working at the same time of the day.

Generally, agricultural employers are also subject to state unemployment taxes, and employers should contact their state workforce agencies to learn the exact requirements.

PAYROLL TAXES

In the United States' income tax system employers are required to withhold a portion of each employee's income and pay it directly to the U.S. Internal Revenue Service. This withholding acts as a prepayment of tax they will owe at the end of the year, as well as a direct payment of certain other taxes.

Payroll tax:
Generally refers to two kinds of taxes: taxes which employers are required to withhold from employees pay, also known as withholding, Pay-As-You-Earn (PAYE) or Pay-As-You-Go (PAYG) tax; or taxes directly related to employing a worker paid from the employer's own funds -- these may be either fixed charges or proportionally linked to an employee's pay.

Payroll taxes include Social Security and Medicare taxes (also known as FICA).

CHAPTER 11

LEGAL

All businesses require legal services in one form or another. This could be from legal advice to establish the company to representation to protect intellectual property. Finding a good lawyer to represent your business is important. Legal services can be obtained at reasonable cost. There are several ways you can approach obtaining legal services.

You can obtain the services of an attorney and pay as you go whenever you need their service.

Another method is to prepay for the service. With this method you pay as low as $9 per month and obtain legal advice, consultation, trial coverage, and coverage in other areas such as marital problems, bankruptcy, real estate matters, etc.

Sources for obtaining legal services include:

Attorney Pages
http://attorneypages.com
Find attorneys that specialize in all types of legal matters in any state.

Find Law
http://www.findlaw.com
Find attorneys that specialize in all types of legal matters in any state.

Just Answer
http://www.justanswer.com/law
Provides Legal Help online

CHAPTER 12

FINANCE

A good business idea cannot survive without adequate financing. All businesses need to be properly capitalized in order to survive and grow. The future entrepreneur has to start by looking at where they put their money. Choosing the right bank to establish your bank account can solve some of your financial problems. Many banks are recognizing small businesses as a market and are offering tailor-made packages to them, which include overdraft protection and credit cards.

Other means of financing include equity and debt financing. These are money obtained from investors (such as Angel investors, venture capitalists, friends & family) and lending institutions (such as banks). Another means of financing is crowd funding. Crowd funding is a means of obtaining financing from donors without incurring debt or giving up equity in your business.

WHERE SHOULD YOU BANK

Where you should bank depends on your type of business and the type of transactions you will be making. For example, if you are in the retail business where at the end of the day you have cash that has to be deposited, then you want to choose a bank that has a branch nearby where you can make your deposits. On the other hand if all of your transactions are done online via online merchant account, then the physical location of the bank is not that important.

If you or your employees will be making ATM transactions locally or when you travel, you should ensure that your bank subscribes to the widely used ATM services.

You should look for banks that reach out to small businesses. These banks offer services such as free business checking, reduced fees on transactions, payroll services for small businesses, overdraft protection, small business credit, free online banking, etc.

You should look for banks that make the process of establishing a small business account easy. It should not take more than five pieces of information to get an account established. Some banks require way too much information and ask for too many documents to be completed before they can start the process. Some banks even go further by inquiring into your credit record before they determine whether or not to give you an account. Those are the ones to avoid.

WHAT DO YOU NEED TO OPEN A BANK ACCOUNT

The basic requirements to open a business bank account include the following:

1. Articles of Incorporation.
2. Federal Employer Income tax Number (FEIN) or SSN
3. Identification
4. Your name, address, phone number, e-mail address and SSN.
5. Business address, phone, fax and e-mail address.

TOP 20 BANKS

See **Appendix F** for the top 20 banks for small businesses.

FINANCING THE BUSINESSS

There are two main types of financing **equity** and **debt.**

Equity Financing:
is money that is received from investors in exchange for a share of ownership in the business. Investors will want anywhere from 10 to 50 percent in a business, depending on the level of investment. With this method of financing you will lose total control in the business. Investors also want a specified return on their investment within a set timeframe. This means that an exit strategy that involves selling the business at a specified timeframe will have to be established in order for them to recoup their investment.

Sources of equity financing include: friends, relatives, employees, customers, angel investors, Venture Capitalists and Small Business Investment Companies (SBIC).

Equity financing is a difficult process. It requires a good business plan and the ability to sell the idea to investors who are not easily convinced. Investors are looking for businesses with good products/services that will grow quickly and also have the right management team. Finding equity investors is a difficult process. You have to make your pitch to many before you find one that is willing to invest.

Equity investors often limit their investments to specific industries. When looking for equity investors search for those who invest in your specific industry.

Below is a link where you can find angel and venture capitalists. *Visit The Small Business Zone Web site (**http://www.sbz1.com**) to see a more extensive list.*

BoogarList
http://www.boogar.com/resources/venturecapital/angels.htm
List of **angel investors and venture capitalists nationwide** from A-Z that you can contact directly.

Debt Financing:
refers to any money that your business borrows and is obliged to pay back. Debt is usually obtained from banks and other traditional lenders, but also may be obtained from other individuals. Debt financing will usually require monthly payments of principal and interest over a fixed period of time.

Types of financial institutions that provide debt financing includes banks, credit unions, consumer finance companies and commercial finance companies.

Entrepreneurs seeking debt financing should ensure that they have a good credit record (700 or above). Entrepreneurs will have their personal credit history examined when applying for a loan if their business has no credit history.

The Small Business Administration (SBA) provides government backed loans to small businesses. However, small businesses must be qualified on the same standards as any other business by a bank first in order to get the SBA back loans. Learn more at www.sba.gov.

There are also institutions that are engaged in providing micro loans to small businesses. These loans start at $2,500 and go as high as $25,000. *Visit the Small Business Zone at http:www.sbz1.com to learn more about these organizations.*

States also have programs that provide debt financing with low interest rates. *Visit the Small Business Zone at **http:www.sbz1.com** (under financing) to learn more about these states programs.*

Crowd Funding:
Crowd funding is a mechanism of financing that was introduced specifically to help small businesses raise capital without incurring debit or giving up equity in the business. Small businesses should try this method first before incurring debt or giving up equity. *Visit the Small Business Zone at **http:www.sbz1.com** (under financing) to learn more about these states programs*

CHAPTER 13

INSURANCE

Every business should have some form of business insurance. This is a way of protecting the organization from unforeseen events such as lawsuits, natural disasters like hurricanes and earthquakes, and man-made disasters for instance theft or destruction to property. Business insurance can be inexpensive or expensive depending on the nature of the business you're in. A small print shop can be inexpensive to insure as opposed to a medical practice which experiences frequent lawsuits and large claims.

Business insurance includes property insurance, liability insurance, health insurance, and bonding insurance.

PROPERTY INSURANCE

Property Insurance: is not mandatory. However, some landlords require their tenants to obtain property insurance. It protects your business against the loss or loss of use of company property. "Property" can include a variety of types: lost income or business interruption, buildings, computers, money and valuable papers.

When shopping for property insurance you should also inquire about the following:

 - *Undamaged stock protection:* covers undamaged items that can no longer be marketed because of damage to related goods

 - *Data or records protection:* covers loss of data or company records

- *Computer virus protection:* covers the loss of data and business through computer viruses

- ***Off-premises property protection:*** extends your
property coverage to include protection at other locations
such as trade shows, fairs, installations, exhibits or any
other place where your company is doing business with
company-owned equipment

  - ***Intangible coverage:*** this includes patents, copyrights
and trademarks.

LIABILITY INSURANCE

Business liability insurance protects your small business in the
event of a lawsuit for personal injury or property damages. It will
usually cover the damages from a lawsuit along with the legal costs.
There are different types of liability insurance. You may purchase
a particular type based on your business needs.

General Liability Insurance: This form of business liability
insurance is the main coverage to protect your business from
events such as injury claims, property damages and advertising
claims. General liability insurance also known as Commercial
General Liability (CGL) may be the only type of business liability
insurance you need depending on your business situation.

Professional Liability Insurance: Business owners providing
services will need to consider having professional liability insurance
known as errors and omissions. This coverage protects your
business against malpractice, errors, negligence and omissions.
Depending on your profession, it may be a legal requirement to
carry such a policy. Doctors require coverage to practice in certain
states. Technology consultants often need coverage in
independent contractor work arrangements.

Product Liability Insurance: Small businesses selling or
manufacturing products should be protected in the event of a
person becoming injured as a result of using the product. The
amount of coverage and the level of risk depend on your business
type. A retailer of scrap book supplies will have far less risks than
a wood stove builder.

BUSINESS OWNERS POLICY (BOP)

BUSINESS OWNER'S POLICIES (BOPs): are insurance packages that provide both property and liability coverage at one affordable premium. These packaged policies are available to most small and medium-size companies and can be a good alternative to purchasing separate policies for liability and property insurance.

Large companies and businesses that are considered high risk usually don't meet the criteria for a BOP. The criteria for BOP eligibility include the size of the premises, the required limits of liability, the type of business and the extent of offsite activity. Premiums for BOP policies are based on similar factors, including business location, financial stability, building construction, security features and fire hazards.

What Does a BOP Cover?
A BOP includes property protection for an office building and its contents as well as other people's property brought into the office building. BOPs cover standard perils, including fire and theft, although certain exclusions apply, such as damage caused by floods and earthquakes.

Under a BOP, a business selects the amount of liability coverage it needs based on its assets. Liability coverage pays for the cost of defending the business in a lawsuit and pays damages if the business is sued for injury or property damage. The liability policy also pays the medical expenses of those injured, other than employees, as a result of business operations.

A BOP provides coverage for both business interruption and replacement costs if an emergency disrupts or destroys the business. Business interruption insurance not only compensates for lost income and the expenses incurred when a company is forced to vacate its premises due to disaster-related damage, but it also covers operating expenses, like payrolls, which continue even when business activities have ceased. Replacement-cost coverage pays to replace damaged or stolen property, equipment and inventory without deducting for depreciation.

In addition to the basic BOP policy, businesses may purchase add-on coverage based on the particular risks associated with the company. For example, a dry cleaner may purchase additional coverage for mechanical breakdown, which would cover the machinery the business relies on. A retailer with numerous employees might carry coverage for employee dishonesty, which covers loss of business property due to embezzlement, fraud or other criminal acts.

When purchasing business insurance it's important to be sure that your company is neither over insured nor underinsured. List all company assets (including property, equipment and inventory) to help you decide the amount of insurance you need. An insurance agent or broker can help you identify risks and determine the type of coverage needed in order to fully protect the company.

HEALTH INSURANCE

The single most expensive benefit offered by employers to employees is health insurance. Health insurance is extremely important to most employees and is therefore a very powerful benefit in recruiting and retaining the best workers. This is health coverage for employees paid for by the employer (with or without some employee contributions). It is a benefit potential employees look for when determining where to seek employment.

Federal law does not mandate employers to provide healthcare for their employees. However, federal law (HIPAA) does prohibit insurance agencies from discriminating against employees and dependents based on their health status.

Small group health insurance provided by insurers is regulated by the states. All states (except for HI) do not mandate employers provide healthcare for their employees. However, some states do mandate that certain types of insurance coverage must be provided if employers choose to provide health insurance to their employees.

In an effort to provide health insurance to those citizens without it, several states recently introduced legislation focused on providing universal health coverage. Check with your **state insurance**

department to understand the current laws in your state and how they might affect small businesses. *(A word of caution: most states' insurance department Web sites are focused on providing information to insurance agencies that they regulate and to individuals).*

Group health insurance plans are categorized as either **indemnity plans** (also known as "traditional indemnity," "fee-for-service" or "FFS" plans) or **managed care plans**.

BONDING INSURANCE

Bonding usually refers to a type of surety guarantee that a specific project, service or act will be financially covered if performance is not complete or satisfactory. Some situations covered by bonding include non-completion of a contracted project or service, cost overruns, not meeting schedules, unsatisfactory quality of work, damage to a customer's property while a project is underway or injury to customer's personnel during work.

For example, projects or services involving construction, home healthcare, electrical contracting, real estate inspection, gardening services, delivery or moving services, etc.

Companies or individuals providing these services customarily secure a bond from a bonding company assuring that if a customer's project is not completed, or is not deemed to have been satisfactorily completed, the bonding company will reimburse the customer for financial loss.

Bonding is required because some customers will not contract work out to companies or individuals that are not bonded.

Bonding fees are charged based on the type of business and financial risk involved. Most bonding companies have special packages for certain types of industries. Pricing and coverage is competitive. You should shop around before deciding on a policy.

Types of Surety Bonds:
There are two types of bonds:

> 1. Contract Bonds (bid, performance, labor and material, payment, indemnity bonds), and

2. License or permit bonds, which are required for many occupations, including contractors.

Below is a link where you can find insurance service providers. *Visit The Small Business Zone Web site (**http://www.sbz1.com**) to see a more extensive list.*

Accredited Surety and Casualty Co., Inc.
http://www.accredited-inc.com
Provides bonding insurance to contractors, agriculture, financial, retail, etc., in all states.

AHM Financial Group, LLC
http://www.ahmins.com
Provides liability, health, property and workers compensation insurance through the U.S.

CHAPTER 14

BUSINESS ADVANTAGE

One way to gain an advantage in business is to take advantage of special zones created by the state and federal governments to give certain types of small businesses a distinct advantage. These zones give small businesses preference in getting government contracts as prime or sub-contractors, tax incentives and incentives such as small business loans. These opportunities are offered by the federal, state and local governments. These zones include:

- 8(a)/ Small Disadvantage Business (SDB)
- Disadvantaged Business Enterprise (DBE)
  Minority Business Enterprise (MBE)
  Women Business Enterprise (WBE)
- Veterans Small Business
- Service Disabled Veteran Owned Business (SDV)
- Hub Zone
- Business Enterprise Zone

8(a)/ SMALL DISADVANTAGE BUSINESS (SDB)

The federal government sets a goal for a certain amount of contracting opportunities to go to Small Disadvantaged Businesses.

The 8(a)/SDB program is a business development program that offers a broad scope of assistance to socially and economically disadvantaged firms; benefits include Small Business Administration backed loans.

8(a)/SDB certification is completed at the federal government level. The Small Business Administration manages this process. The application process involves revealing many details about you and your business finances.

SDB (Small Disadvantaged Business) certification strictly pertains to **benefits in federal procurement**. 8(a) firms automatically qualify for SDB certification.

According to statutory language governing the program, a business owner is considered disadvantaged if he can be certified as socially and economically disadvantaged.

A business owner(s) is presumed to be socially disadvantaged if he is a member of a minority group. He must then prove economic disadvantage by providing evidence to show that his personal net worth does not exceed the applicable thresholds ($750,000) -- 51% of the company must be owned by the minority.

It takes 90 days for 8(a) certification and 75 days for SDB certification.

You can find a certification guide at:
https://sba8a.symplicity.com/applicants/guide

DISADVANTAGED BUSINESS ENTERPRISE (DBE)
MINORITY BUSINESS ENTERPRISE (MBE)
WOMEN BUSINESS ENTERPRISE (WBE)

Minority Business Enterprise (MBE), Women Business Enterprise (WBE) and Disadvantage Business Enterprise (DBE) are programs implemented at the state, city and county level. These certifications provide small businesses with the opportunity of being considered ahead of other businesses when it comes to doing business with the state, city or county. In some cases these organizations may also receive financial assistance in the form of low interest rate loans.

State certification for the most part is managed by the states' Department of Transportation. Many states have what is called a unified application process, which enables you to file one application and be certified with other municipalities (e.g. city and counties). Also, if you already have a 8(a)/SDB certification many states have a streamlined process for DBE certification.

Many cities do not have a Disadvantaged Business Certification program. Be aware that some municipalities require a filing fee. The processing time and paperwork required depends on the municipality.

*Visit The Small Business Zone Web site (**http://www.sbz1.com**) to see states and other municipalities Web sites for DB E/WBE and MBE.*

VETERANS SMALL BUSINESS

There are many benefits to being recognized as a Veteran Small Business. They include financial help and preferences in government contracting.

Veteran Small Business certification is mainly a function of the federal government (Veteran's Administration).

Visit this Web site to learn more about Veterans Small Business assistance.
http://www.vetbiz.gov/library/library.htm

SERVICE DISABLED VETERAN OWNED BUSINESS (SDV)

Service Disabled Veteran certification is mainly a federal government program; however, some states do have their own SDV programs. There are several benefits to being certified as a Service Disabled Veteran including set aside contracting opportunities and short procurement lead times.

To learn more visit the Association for Service Disabled Veterans Web site. **http://www.asdv.org/index2.cfm**

GSA Service Disabled Web site:
http://www.gsa.gov/portal/content/105166

HUB ZONE

Historically Underutilized Businesses (HUB) Zones are areas designated by the federal government as being economically depressed. In an effort to stimulate growth in those areas the government provides incentives for businesses to setup and operate in those areas. The program is managed by the Small Business Administration (SBA). The SBA provides HUB Zone Certifications.

You can view the designated HUB Zone areas by using the link at the SBA's Web site:
https://eweb1.sba.gov/hubzone/internet/index.cfm

BUSINESS ENTERPRISE ZONE

The Enterprise Zone Program designates areas within the states that are considered economically depressed and are targeted for economic development. In order to spur economic development in those targeted areas the states (and sometimes local municipalities) offer tax incentives to businesses to setup and operate in those areas. Not all states have a Business Enterprise Zone program.

These are by and far state programs even though some states receive support from the federal government for their programs.

Economic incentives include:

- Tax credit for creating new jobs
- Sales tax exemptions
- Use tax exemptions
- Income tax credit
- Franchise tax credit
- Preferential treatment when bidding on government contracts
- Property tax abatement
- New equipment taxis abatement
- Etc.

The Business Enterprise Zone program has different names depending on the state. Some are called the Economic Development Zone, Empire Program, Business Development Zone, Economic Zone, etc.

*Visit The Small Business Zone Web site (**http://www.sbz1.com**) to see states Web sites for Enterprise Zone programs.*

GSA SCHEDULE

If you want the federal government as your customer BE SURE TO GET LISTED IN THE GSA SCHEDULE. Under the GSA Schedules program (also referred to as Multiple Award Schedules and Federal Supply Schedules Program), GSA establishes long-term government-wide contracts with commercial firms to provide access to over 10 million commercial supplies and services that can be ordered directly from GSA Schedule contractors or through the GSA Advantage online shopping and ordering system.

You can find access to the GSA Schedule via the link below:
http://www.gsa.gov

CHAPTER 15

GOVERNMENT CONTRACTING

Making the federal or state government one of your clients can be lucrative for your business. The federal and state governments buy all kinds of products and services from the private industry. You can set your business up to be a vendor to the government by making sure you understand the system and follow the process to become a vendor.

CONTRACTING WITH THE FEDERAL GOVERNMENT

Contracting with the federal government is divided between purchases under $25,000 and purchases over $25,000.

Purchases under $25,000 are accomplished on what is called a **GSA SCHEDULES PROGRAM**. This is where vendors are pre-qualified and placed on an Authorized Vendor List for agencies in the federal government to do business with.

Purchases over $25,000 are conducted through the **FEDBIZOPS** Web site (**https://www.fbo.gov**) and serve as the single point of entry for all federal government procurement opportunities. Through this Web site the government puts out a Request for Proposal (RFP), or a Request for Information (RFI), and vendors respond (place a bid) to the RFP or RFI. Based on those responses the government selects the best candidate for the contract (usually the lowest bidder). A contract can be for a single year or multi-year. There are also **Set Aside** programs where contracts are reserved for only minority and women owned businesses to bid on. Information on whether or not the contract is a **Set Aside** listed in the RFP.

STATE GOVERNMENT CONTRACTING OPPORTUNITIES

Like the federal government, the state governments also have a centralized procurement system in place. Some states' procurement systems not only manage procurement for the state, but also for the major cities within the state.

Also, like the federal government, the states divide contracting based on the dollar amount of the products or service being procured. The breakdown is different from state to state. Therefore, in addition to responding to RFPs be sure to get on the states' vendor list for other contracting opportunities.

*Visit The Small Business Zone Web site (**http://www.sbz1.com**) to see states' Web sites for contracting opportunities.*

SUBCONTRACTING OPPORTUNITIES

Subcontracting is another way to increase revenues through government contracting. If you are not able to become the primary contractor on a project you may still be able to get in on the project by becoming a subcontractor to the primary contractor. Use the Small Business Administration (SBA) subcontracting resource to take advantage of subcontracting (**http://web.sba.gov/subnet/search/index.cfm**).

*Visit The Small Business Zone Web site (**http://www.sbz1.com**) to see more contracting opportunities.*

MUST DO

Before any vendor can do business with the government they must be registered in the System of Award Management (SAM) database. The service is free.

SAM (System of Award Management):
https://www.sam.gov/portal/public/sam

DUNS NUMBER

In order to be registered in the SAM database and do business with the government all vendors must have a Data Universal Numbering System (DUNS) Number. The DUNS Number is assigned by Dun & Bradstreet, Inc.

The DUNS Number is a unique nine-digit identification number, for each physical location of your business. The service is free.

Register for the DUNS Number at this web address:
http://fedgov.dnb.com/webform/displayHomePage.do;jses sionid=D965FB8ED3CCD73FBDB70CE3F94B3439

CHAPTER 16

DOMAIN NAMES

Why do you need a domain name for your business?

The answer is simple: a domain name allows you to setup a business Web site. If you do not have a business Web site and e-mail address your business will not be taken seriously. When people are looking for a product or service the first research tool they use is the web. Therefore, not only will your business not be taken seriously, but you're also losing out on prime opportunities.

A Web address gives your customers and potential customers an opportunity to learn about what you have to offer and place orders 24/7 from anywhere in the world.

Registering your domain name should be one of the first things you do before registering your business. When you register your business you should consider the opportunity for others to benefit from your business name and register the appropriate **TOP LEVEL** domain names in order to prevent this. For example, if you register your domain only as **www.blueballs.com,** but did not register the **www.blueballs.net, www.blueballs.org, www.blueballs.biz, www.blueballs.tv,** then someone can come along and register those names and benefit from the popularity of your name by luring web goers to their sites.

The following are referred to as **TOP LEVEL** domain names:
- .com = commerce
- .net = unrestricted use
- .org = organization
- .biz = business
- .tv = videos
- .info = informational sites
- .gov = government
- .mobi = mobile device services
- .edu = education
- .mil = military
- .name = families & individuals
- etc.

You register your domain name through companies authorized to perform such function. ICANN (**Internet Corporation for Assigned Names and Numbers**) is the world body that authorizes companies worldwide to perform such function.

Below is a list of some of the companies in the U.S. authorized to perform domain name registration. *Visit The Small Business Zone Web site (**http://www.sbz1.com**) for a more extensive list.*

http://www.godaddy.com
http://www.networksolutions.com
http://www.register.com
http://www.google.com
http://www.yahoo.com

CHAPTER 17

INTERNET CONNECTION

Every business needs a connection to the Internet. An Internet connection can be used for many purposes including managing your Web site, accessing e-mails, conducting research, placing orders, accepting and processing orders, banking and reducing your telephone bills via VOIP (Voice Over Internet Protocol) for your phone service, etc.

You have many choices for your Internet connection services. Gone are the days of the slow dial-up modem connections. Today you can get high-speed (Broadband) connections at very inexpensive rates (less than $50 per month) for your office. Below is a description of the different types of connection services. What service you can use will depend on what is available in your area. In some areas you may have the option to use several types of connection services, while in other areas you may only have the option of having one type of service.

BROADBAND CONNECTIONS

This is a high-speed connection to the Internet via DSL, Cable, Satellite, ISDN, T-1, Mobile broadband/Wi-Fi, etc. (dial-up modem is not considered Broadband).

DSL (Digital Subscriber Line):
This is a high-speed connection that uses the telephone line in your office to provide a much greater connection speed than dial-up service. Prices are usually cheaper or comparable to cable.

Cable:
The same cable that brings the signal to your TV also can be used to provide a high-speed connection to the Internet. Service providers that provide cable TV service also provide the Internet connection service through the same cable. The price for cable connection is usually a bit more than for DSL.

Satellite:
This service requires you to have a dish and box that send and receive the signal from the satellite. This type of service is affected by heavy clouds and anything that obstructs the view of the satellite dish. The price is usually three to five times more than DSL.

ISDN (Integrated Services Digital Network):
This service is provided through a special land line that runs to a location in your building. A connection is made when any user on the network opens their Internet browser; this is a very expensive method -- much more expensive than satellite.

T-1:
This service is provided through a special land line that runs to a location in your building. It provides faster connection speeds than DSL, Cable, Satellite, ISDN, and Wi-Fi. However, it is more expensive than all of them.

Mobile Broadband/Wi-Fi:
This service is provided through a wireless high-speed network card that you plug into the PC card slot in your laptop. The average price for the card is $300. The average monthly service charge is $59.99.

Dial-up: (not Broadband)
This involves the use of a modem in your computer that is connected to a phone line. You make a connection through your modem then launch your Internet browser to connect to the Internet.

MiFi
A compact wireless router that serves as a mobile Wi-Fi hotspot. It provides broadband connectivity through a cellular network. It can allow multiple computers (normally 5) to connect to the Internet simultaneously. You pay a monthly subscription fee to a cellular company such as Sprint, Verizon or T-Mobile.

INTERNET SERVICE PROVIDERS (ISP)

Below is a list of some Internet service providers. *Visit The Small Business Zone Web site (**http://www.sbz1.com**) for a more extensive list.*

http://www.earthlink.biz/highspeed/index.jsp
http://www.att.com
http://comcast.com

CHAPTER 18

WEB SITE CREATION

When it comes to setting up your Web site you have several options:

1. DO-IT-YOURSELF SOFTWARE
2. DO-IT-YOURSELF TEMPLATE
3. HIRE A WEB DESIGNER

DO-IT-YOURSELF SOFTWARE

Below is a list of some Do-It-Yourself software. *Visit The Small Business Zone Web site (**http://www.sbz1.com**) for a more extensive list.*

Adobe Dreamweaver CS3
PrintShop Web Designer
OpenLaszlo

DO-IT-YOURSELF TEMPLATE

Another approach is would be to take advantage of online templates to design your Web site.

Below is a list of some online templates services. Visit The Small Business Zone Web site (**http://www.sbz1.com**) for a more extensive list.

Afforda
http://domains.afforda.com/sitebuilder.php?type=sblite
Utilize the template anywhere. **COST: Starts at $1.25 per month.**

1&1
http://order.1and1.com/An online template that you subscribe to. **COST: Starts at $8.99 per month.**

AIT Inc.

http://templatestore.aitcom.net/

Download and use the template anywhere. **COST: Starts at $9.95 per month.**

HIRE A WEB DESIGNER

The best approach to finding a Web designer is to take advantage of a Web designer directory service, like the ones listed below. These services allow you to submit your project and have Web designers bid on it. Therefore, you will pay the best price for the service.

Web designers charge a fee to update your page. They give you a certain amount of free updates per month then charge a fee for any changes needed after that.

Below is a list of some Web designer services. *Visit The Small Business Zone Web site (**http://www.sbz1.com**) for a more extensive list.*

Guru

http://www.guru.com

A directory listing Web designers. You can request quotes from specific designers.

Freelance Designers

http://www.freelancedesigners.com

Submit a quote request and receive responses for Web design, logo design and graphics design.

CHAPTER 19

PHONE/FAX

Phone and fax services are essential means of communication for every business. Competition in the phone industry has resulted in more choices and better prices for phone/fax services.
Voice and fax service is provided by a host of companies.
Knowing what features are provided in their services will help you to make the right choice.

Improvements in technology have made it possible for the small business to appear like a big business to both their loyal and potential customers at very inexpensive prices. For example, for less than $50 a month you can have a business phone and fax service that includes an answering service with all the bells and whistles. Review the type of services you can have and see a list of vendors below.

LAND LINE

This is the actual physical phone line that comes into your building. Your phone connects to this line via phone jack that goes into the wall.

WIRELESS

This service does not require a land line; it relies on radio waves.

VOIP (VOICE OVER INTERNET PROTOCOL)

This is a phone or fax service that requires your Cable, DSL or Satellite (broadband) connection in order to work. A VOIP device connects to your broadband connection and your phone/fax connects to the VOIP device.

VIRTUAL FAX

A fax service that does not require a land line; it operates over the Internet. When someone sends a fax to you they send it to a regular fax number, which routes the fax to a virtual location on the Internet. The fax is then sent to your e-mail account. Another option is to have it go to a dedicated online fax site that you log into then view, print or download your fax.

NETWORK FAX

This is when software is installed on a computer in your office which allows the computer to act as a fax machine (fax server) -- the computer will keep an electronic copy of all faxes. The software includes features that allow other users in your office network to send and receive fax from their respective computers by allowing them to connect to the central fax computer (fax server).

PBX (PRIVATE BRANCH EXCHANGE)

This is a small, box-like device that you plug your phone line into and configure it to act as an automated receptionist. It will route calls to the appropriate divisions of your company when the user dials the respective extensions; it can hold calls in a queue and can be configured to forward calls as well as containing other useful features.

VIRTUAL PBX (PRIVATE BRANCH EXCHANGE)

Provides the same services as the PBX above, however this is done over the Internet instead of buying and installing the PBX device in your office.

Below is a list of some phone/fax services providers. Visit The Small Business Zone Web site (**http://www.sbz1.com**) for a more extensive list.

Grasshopper
http://grasshopper.com/
Grasshopper provides a virtual phone answering and forwarding system and it requires no traditional phone lines. When you sign up for the service you are assigned an 800 number that you provide to customers as your contact number. You provide the phone to your employees in addition to telling the service what calls to transfer to your employees' phones. It also allows you to set pre-recorded messages for customers to select a number to go to different departments and leave messages when someone is not available to take a call. **COST: Start at $9.95 per month.**

eFax
http://home.efax.com/s/r/gen-efax-plus5?VID=33675

Send and receive fax through your e-mail. **COST: Start at $10.00 per month.**

CHAPTER 20

FINDING A LOCATION

Finding the right location for your business could mean the difference between being successful or unsuccessful. Finding a location does not have to be a painstaking event. Most of the leg work can be conducted on the Web. You can quickly find out what is available in a given area by researching the Web, then you can do a drive by and take a look at the building. There are organizations that will help you find a location at no cost (see below).

When it comes to choosing a type of office space you have several options. You can have dedicated office space, serviced/shared office space or virtual office space.

DEDICATED OFFICE SPACE

A dedicated office space is a lease/rented office space dedicated to your business only and is not shared with others. You are responsible for any services such as secretarial services, office management services, fax and answering service, etc.

SERVICED/SHARED OFFICE SPACE

Service or shared office space is a leased/rented office space whereby certain services are provided for you by the lease organization, including secretarial, office management, fax and answering service, etc. You also share resources, like conference rooms, with other organizations in the building. There are no long-term lease agreements. You pay on a month-to-month basis. In addition to security deposits there is usually a setup fee for the serviced/shared office lease/rental.

VIRTUAL OFFICE

A virtual office service is designed for those who need access to office space and business services on an as-needed basis. These are usually used by those who work from home or somewhere else and want to project an image of a larger, more professional organization with an office in a prestigious location. Generally these programs offer a mailing address, several hours of private office or conference room use per month, telephone answering, and courier and concierge services. There is usually a setup fee for virtual office lease/rental.

Below is a list of some search services for finding office spaces. *Visit The Small Business Zone Web site (**http://www.sbz1.com**) for a more extensive list.*

SOS Worldwide
http://www.sos-worldwide.com/serviced-offices/usa/about_us.html
Provide furnished office space location services throughout the US. Services include reception and telephone answering services, secretarial support, conference and meeting facilities, video conferencing and high speed internet access; provides virtual offices. **COST: free.**

HQ
http://www.hq.com/go/officespace
Provides locator service to help you find office space in nationwide and internationally. **COST: free.**

CHAPTER 21

MAILBOX

Many business owners utilize a mailing address that is different from the actual place of business. If you want to do the same for your business you have several choices:

PHYSICAL MAILBOX

This is an actual physical location where your mail is dropped off and you can go there and retrieve your mail.

VIRTUAL MAILBOX

This is a location that receives your mail for you, scans it and uploads it to a virtual location where you can access it over the Internet. You can then decide whether to discard, hold or have your mail forward to you.

PHYSICAL MAILBOX AND VIRTUAL MAILBOX

Some sites provide both physical mailbox and virtual mailbox service.

Mailbox service providers also provide other services such as being able to accept certified mail from UPS, USPS, FEDEX, DHL, etc. They also provide shipping services such as UPS, USPS, FEDEX and DHL.

Prices range from $72 - $360 dollars annually for mailboxes at a physical location and $9.95 monthly for a virtual mailbox.

Below is a list of some mailbox service providers. *Visit The Small Business Zone Web site (**http://www.sbz1.com**) for a more extensive list.*

USPS (The United States Postal Service)
http://www.usps.com/receive/businesssolutions/poboxserv
ice.htm

Have your mail delivered to a local U.S. post office mailbox location. **COST: Starts at $42 for every six months.**

The UPS Store
http://www.theupsstore.com/products/proandser.html
Have your mail delivered to a physical post office mailbox location. You can call to check if you have new mail (operates nationwide).

US Mail1
http://usamail1.com
Have your mail delivered to a physical post office mailbox location. You then access the mailbox over the Internet and determine which mail to discard or keep. The mail you keep can be delivered to you (based in Monsey, New York).

CHAPTER 22

OFFICE FURNITURE

There are several ways to furnish your office.

BUY NEW

You can buy brand new furnishings for your office via online stores or retail stores.

BUY USED

You can buy furnishings that have been previously used via online stores or retail stores.

RENT/LEASE

You can rent/lease for short or long-term usage. With this option you pay a monthly fee for the equipment you use. If you can't come up with the total amount of cash upfront to furnish your office, this is a good option.

Below is a list of office furniture providers. *Visit The Small Business Zone Web site (**http://www.sbz1.com**) for a more extensive list.*

Overstock.com
http://www.overstock.com/Home-Garden/Home-Office-Furniture/712/cat.html
Sells office furniture via retail stores and the Internet, based in California and Texas. Also provides delivery service.

Aaron Rentals
http://www.aaronrents.com
Rents office furniture via retail stores nationwide.

eBay
http://www.ebay.com
Bid on furniture online at the eBay furniture auction site. You may have to pay for shipment or pick up the item yourself.

CHAPTER 23

STORAGE

You may need a site to temporarily store supplies or office equipment. There are reasonably priced solutions for your storage needs.

Below is a list of some storage service providers. *Visit The Small Business Zone Web site (**http://www.sbz1.com**) for a more extensive list.*

UHALL
http://www.uhaul.com/storage/
Provides storage service. **COST: Average $69 for 5x5x8**

Public Storage
http://www.publicstorage.com/?pid=webmetrogoogle
Provides storage service nationwide. **COST: Starts at $57 for a 5x5 size space.**

Vanlines
http://www.vanlines.com/storage/self_storage.html
A search service that can give you the address and phone number of any storage facility in your area. **COST: The search service is free.**

CHAPTER 24

LEASING

Instead of having to come up with a large sum of money to buy equipment you need to setup and operate the business, you have the option of leasing it. This allows you to own and operate the equipment by making small monthly payments, instead of having to pay the cost upfront.

WHAT IS LEASING

A lease grants the use of assets for a specified time and payment. Whoever owns the lease and lends is called the *lessor,* while the borrower is called the *lessee*. Leases are usually for a period of 1-6 years and it usually involves a simple, one-page application process. The amounts range from $2,000 to $35,000,000. The payment terms will depend on the lessee's credit record. Most lessors will lend even though you may have a poor credit history. Some lessors only service certain industries, while others service all.

TYPES OF LEASING

One Dollar Purchase Option:
At the end of the lease period the lessee gets to own the equipment for a payment of $1. The monthly payments are usually higher than other types of leases. Since it qualifies as a purchase you can write off $24,000 in the year the lease begins.

True Lease (or Fair Market Value):
Allows the lessee to purchase the equipment at fair market value at the end of the lease. Each payment is written off as an expense.

Fixed Price Purchase Option:
A fixed price is established for ownership at the end of the lease (normally 10% balloon payment). The regular monthly payments are usually lower.

WHY LEASE

Tax Purposes:
You can claim lease payment for tax purposes.

Availability of Assets:
Gain access to equipment for a small monthly fee instead of having to finance the total cost upfront, thereby having your assets available to grow business.

Access to Equipment:
Leasing provides access to equipment even though you can't afford the total cost upfront.

Reducing the Risk of Obsolescence:
Since you do not own the equipment you don't have to worry about disposing of old equipment or lose out on the depreciating value of it.

THE LEASING PROCESS

1. You can choose the type of equipment you need from the equipment supplier you would like it from.

2. Submit a lease application for processing. In most cases this is a simple one-form application.

3. Upon credit review and approval, a lease agreement is sent to you for signing. Most agencies will provide a response within 48 hours.

4. Overnight the signed lease agreement back to them.

5. The equipment supplier delivers and installs the equipment.

6. Once they verify you have received the equipment and are satisfied with it, the equipment supplier is paid in full (100% financing, includes the costs of delivery, installation, software and other service charges).

LEASING COMPANIES

Below is a list of some leasing service providers. *Visit The Small Business Zone Web site (**http://www.sbz1.com**) for a more extensive list.*

1ST Equipment Leasing Co.
http://www.acceleratedleasing.com

Provides leasing services to businesses of all sizes. Approval decision within hours. **Finance up to $75,000**.

All Options Leasing
http://equipment.alloptions.com/index.asp?Camp=Leasing Home

Provides free directory search service. Submit quote request and receive multiple quotes. Finances from $25,000 to $20,000,000.

Access Equipment Leasing
http://www.equipment-leasing.org/equipment-lease.html

Provides leasing services to businesses of all sizes.

CHAPTER 25

BARCODE

Barcodes are required to identify specific products. Each type of product is required to have its own barcode. Barcodes allow for the item to be tracked in shipment and identified at the Point of Sale (POS).

You need barcodes if you are producing and selling a product that will be stocked and sold in a retail store.

On the Web you will find many organizations offering barcode issuing services, however all barcode issuing emanates from GS1. **http://www.gs1.org/productssolutions/barcodes/need_a_ba r_code.html**

A one-time fee based on your annual revenues is required. This could start at $750.

There is also an annual maintenance fee which starts at under $150.

Visit the "Frequently Asked Questions" page and find answers to questions. **http://www.gs1.org/productssolutions/barcodes/request/in dex.php**

Once you obtain your barcode you will need to print them for use. You can approach this in three ways. You can **purchase pre-printed barcode labels, the barcode printer** or if you are outsourcing production **send the barcode information to the outsourcing vendor** for them to print it directly onto your product.

PRE PRINTED BARCODE SERVICE

Below is a list of some barcode service providers. *Visit The Small Business Zone Web site (**http://www.sbz1.com**) for a more extensive list.*

Dynamic Barcode Systems
http://www.dynamicbarcode.com/preprinted.htm

ID Lab, Inc.
http://www.idlabelinc.com

PURCHASE BARCODE EQUIPMENT

Below is a list of vendors that provide barcode equipment. *Visit The Small Business Zone Web site (**http://www.sbz1.com**) for a more extensive list.*

WASP Barcode Technologies
http://www.waspbarcode.com/printers/default.asp

eLabeling
http://www.elabeling.com/coso.html

CHAPTER 26

SHIPPING

Conducting business involves sending and receiving packages, sending and receiving supplies, moving into an office, moving the office from one location to another, etc. These are resources that can help you with your shipping and moving needs.

Your business will need national or international shippers, depending the nature of your business.

SHIPPING SMALL PACKAGES

These services allow you to create a business account and manage your shipment over the Internet. You can pay for shipment and print labels. In some cases you can even schedule a pickup once the package is ready for shipment. Rates vary from shipper to shipper depending on the location, size of the package and how quickly you want to have it delivered.

Below is a list of vendors that provide shipment of small packages. *Visit The Small Business Zone Web site (**http://www.sbz1.com**) for a more extensive list.*

UPS
http://www.ups.com/content/us/en/bussol/smallbiz/index.html

FEDEX
http://www.fedex.com/us

DHL
http://www.dhl-usa.com/home/home.asp

SHIPPING LARGE ITEMS

For big items that the U.S. Postal Service, FEDEX, UPS or DHL will not accept because they are too large you have to use independent carriers. They provide shipment for the big items that no one else wants to ship. The best way to find good shipping deals is through SEARCH SERVICES. These services provide the best opportunity to get the best deal available for you. Their databases contain thousands of shippers. You can input a quote request and receive instant feedback from multiple shippers on your inquiry.

Below is a list of vendors that provide shipment of large items. *Visit The Small Business Zone Web site (**http://www.sbz1.com**) for a more extensive list.*

Freight Center
http://www.freightcenter.com/?source=freight
Serves as a central point for finding the best rates and scheduling freight transportation. This source normally provides a better rate than you would receive dealing directly with the shipper. Use of this service is free.

UShip
http://www.uship.com/shipping/freight
Serves as a central point for finding the best rates and scheduling freight transportation. This source also has better rates. Use of this service is also free.

DO-IT-YOURSELF MOVING – RENT A TRUCK

If you prefer to do your own moving you can rent a truck and move yourself. The rates depends on the size of the vehicle, how long you will be using it for and how many miles you will travel.

Below is a list of vendors that provide truck rental service. *Visit The Small Business Zone Web site (**http://www.sbz1.com**) for a more extensive list.*

Budget Rental
http://www.budgettruck.com/Home.aspx?partnerid=428

UHAUL
http://www.uhaul.com

Penske
http://www.pensketruckrental.com

DO-IT-YOURSELF MOVING – LABORERS

Moving can be a labor intensive task. You should find reliable movers that will show up on time and get the job done professionally which will save time and headaches. There are many organizations across the country that provides such a service. You can rent as many laborers as you need for as long as you need by the hour.

Below is a list of vendors that provide laborers. *Visit The Small Business Zone Web site (**http://www.sbz1.com**) for a more extensive list.*

Easy Movers
http://www.easymovinghelp.com
$50 per hour for a two-man team. Minimum of 4 hours.

Emove
http://movinghelp.emove.com
A search service that finds moving helpers in your area that provide labor to help you pack/unpack, load, unload, etc.

DO-IT-YOURSELF MOVING – RENT AND PACK CONTAINER FOR MOVEMENT

There are also moving services that allow you to rent a container and pack it, then have the movers pick it up and ship it or put it in storage. This is another method of moving your goods or business.

Below is a list of vendors that provide container services. *Visit The Small Business Zone Web site (**http://www.sbz1.com**) for a more extensive list.*

Moving 411
http://www.movers411.com/self_service_movers.html

Door-to-Door
http://www.doortodoor.com/?utm_id=1070

CHAPTER 27

IMPORT/EXPORT

We live in a global economy where customers and supplies can be found all around the world. A business can take advantage of overseas markets that can provide cheaper materials needed for production. You must also take into consideration that in today's global economy it is easy to sell a product to a domestic customer as it is to an international customer.

The Department of Commerce is the principal government agency responsible for managing the nation's import and export function. Detailed information about what is required to conduct an import and export business is found on their Web site.

Department of Commerce Web site
http://www.export.gov
The U.S. Department of Commerce should be your starting point; it provides valuable information regarding all aspects of importing and exporting.

Importing and Exporting requires the use of **FORWARDERS or BROKERS** to ship and clear your product through customs. Use the link below to find out more about what FORWARDERS do.
http://www.export.gov/logistics/eg_main_018144.asp

Use this link to find FORWARDERS/BROKERS
http://www.forwarders.com

CHAPTER 28

SUPPLIERS & MANUFACTURERS

If you are going to manufacture a product you need suppliers and perhaps manufacturers if you intend to outsource the manufacturing of the product. Supplies and manufacturers can be found all over the world. If you are looking to create a product at the lowest cost possible then you should do a comparison between domestic and international sources.

When working with suppliers and manufacturers from overseas you should pay particular attention to quality and safety. Ensure that suppliers and manufacturers meet U.S. specifications and standards for products sold in the United States. You do not want to discover that a product does not meet U.S. safety standards after it is on the market. Product recall and battles with your suppliers and manufacturers can be very costly. You definitely want to avoid them.

There are many databases on the Web that you can use to find manufacturers or suppliers for the product you are attempting to develop.

Below is a list of resources for finding suppliers and manufacturers. *Visit The Small Business Zone Web site* (**http://www.sbz1.com**) *for a more extensive list.*

Alibaba
http://www.alibaba.com
Find manufacturers and suppliers for all products anywhere in the world. **COST: use of this service is free.**

Thomas Register
http://www.thomasnet.com
Find manufacturers and suppliers for all products anywhere in the world. **COST: use of this service is free.**

Trade Key
http://www.tradekey.com/c_manufacturers/

This is a trusted site for buyers to find manufacturers and suppliers worldwide. Create an account and post a buy request and get feedback from competing manufacturers/suppliers. Get the most competitive prices. **COST: use of this service is free.**

CHAPTER 29

COPIERS

Having your own copier in your place of business is a lot cheaper in the long run than having to run to Kinkos or other print shops every time you need something copied. Copiers come in all sizes and can be obtained at a very low cost.

There are several options available when it comes to getting copiers for your business.

Purchase:
You can purchase a copier and own it outright. This requires coming up with the total cost upfront. A common concern here would be depreciation.

Lease:
You can lease a copier and receive all the benefits of leasing. You do not have to come up with the total cost upfront. Leasing requires signing a contract and obtaining financing. With this option you wouldn't have to worry about depreciation.

Rent:
Pay on a monthly basis. There is no long-term contract and you don't have to worry about financing and depreciation.

What to look for when choosing a Copier:

Maintenance Contract:
The printer will break sooner or later. How do you get it fixed when that happens? Be sure to consider the cost of a maintenance contract.

Cost of Supplies:
The cost of the ink toner varies from one type of printer to another. Be sure to inquire about what it would cost to replace an ink cartridge and factor that into the overall operating cost of the copier.

Speed/Volume:

How fast a copier can copy pages should be considered. If you are planning on making a large amount of copies then you want a copier that can produce the most volume amount of copies in a minute. For example:

- High Volume: over 50cpm (copies per minute)
- Medium Volume: over 33cpm
- Low Volume: less than 33cpm

Capacity:

Look for the capacity of the paper tray and the type of paper it can handle (for example, does it hold only 50 sheets of paper versus 150 sheets of paper?). Can it handle letters, legal, A4, etc.

Toner Yield:

How many pages can you copy before having to change the toner cartridge? The more copies you can make before having to change the toner cartridge the cheaper the cost per copy. For example, some machines allow you to make 33,000 copies before having to change the toner cartridge.

Below is a list of vendors that provide copier equipment. *Visit The Small Business Zone Web site (**http://www.sbz1.com**) for a more extensive list.*

Coast-to-Coast
http://www.ctcstl.com/services.html
New and refurbish copiers (black, white and color). Provides warranty service on copiers.

Copier Superstore
http://www.copiersuperstore.com/all-copiers.html
Sells new copiers (black, white and color). Provides Warranty service on copiers.

CHAPTER 30

CHECKING ON BUSINESSES

Every business uses the services of other businesses which include office supplies, furniture, cleaning supplies, raw materials for your product, production equipment, legal, finance, consultation, tax preparation, employee services, cleaning, moving and much more.

If you are going to utilize the services of other businesses or take on a client, it is incumbent upon you to find out if they are the right ones to do business with. There are resources available to you for gathering background information on potential vendors or clients.

Make use of the Better Business Bureau (BBB) to find out and analyze complaints against an organization:

BETTER BUSINESS BUREAU (BBB)

Check out a business to see how many complaints are being filed against the organization and how quickly they are resolving them. **COST: Free.** Visit the BBB at: **http://search.bbb.org**

DUNN & BRADSTREET (D&B)

The Dun and Bradstreet (D&B) business verification service is another tool you can use to check on other organizations you are considering doing business with. D&B maintains a database of organizations that can be used to verify the existence of a business entity.
COST: Free trial service monthly rates starts at $45

Visit D&B at:
http://smallbusiness.dnb.com

LOOKUP STATES DATABASES

The states maintain a database of all businesses registered in that state. You can use them to check on businesses you are considering doing business with.

See **Appendix G** for individual state Web addresses and their databases.

CHECK THE CREDIT HISTORY OF AN ORGANIZATION

Here are other resources you can use to check on businesses.

Credit.net
http://www.credit.net/ag_freereport_mailform.asp?si=
Verify the credit history of businesses.

KnowX
http://www.knowx.com/exp/search.jsp?
Verify the credit history of businesses. Buy individual reports on a one-time basis or subscribe on a monthly basis.
COST: Starts at $1.50

CHAPTER 31

EXIT STRATEGY

There comes a point in the life of a business when you have to make an exit. An exit can take on different forms like:

1. Succession planning
2. Sell the business
3. Initial Public Offering (IPO)
4. Closing the business

SUCCESSION PLANNING

Succession planning is the process of identifying, training and mentoring key individuals to assume future leadership roles in the organization should a business owner become disabled, die unexpectedly or retire. Those key players could be from inside or outside of the organization.

Succession Planning Steps:

1. Establish your goals
2. Chose a successor
3. Establish a succession timeframe
4. Establish a training program and timeline
5. Prepare for your exit
6. Install your successor

SELLING THE BUSINESS

Consider the following when selling your business:

1. **Establish your objectives** by specifying the end result of the transaction, what is the minimum price you are willing to accept.
2. **Time the sale** of your business to gain as much tax advantage as possible.
3. **Legal and ethical issues:** be prepared to give full disclosure to the buyer in order to avoid any legal entanglements later on.
4. **How can you add value to the business before selling?**

- Improve your assets
- Clean up potential liabilities

5. **Determine who are you want to sell to:** Do you want to sell to employees, family members, investors or the public (as in Initial Public Offering).

INITIAL PUBLIC OFFERING (IPO)

IPO (Initial Public Offering): This is the process of selling shares/stocks that are privately held to new investors (public or private investors) for the first time.

Companies that trade on stock exchanges such as the NASDAQ, NYSE and AMEX are publicly traded companies. Their stocks are bought and sold through these exchanges to any member of the public or investment firms.

Examples of publicly traded companies include Microsoft, IBM, Apple, Inc., Ford Motor Company, General Motors, Pepsi, Coca Cola, The Wall Street Journal and countless others.

Requirements for going public:

See the SEC's requirements for going public at:
http://www.sec.gov/answers/comppublic.htm

Any company, including foreign companies, can go public. It isn't necessary to have been in business for a certain amount of time.

There are no revenue or asset requirements for going public. However, some underwriters do require that your company generates a certain minimum amount of revenues.

You need a good management team and have your financials audited.

You also need a good outside team which includes your IPO consultants, accountants, attorneys, underwriters and PR specialists.

Depending on the exchange (NASDAQ, OTCBB, NYSE, AMEX) that you want to trade on you will have to satisfy any requirement they may have.

Steps involved in going public:

1. Hire attorneys and accountants (management team) that will advise and guide you through the process.
2. Have your attorneys and accountants prepare a registration statement.
3. Set your IPO date.
4. Submit the registration statement to the SEC and other regulatory bodies.
5. Assemble a management team (accountants, lawyers, etc.) and have them shop your company to stock brokers who will sell your stock to public investors.
6. The blackout period: from the time of filing with the SEC to a period after stock start trading (25 days) when the company is not allowed to make public comments, valuations and earnings estimates.
7. Launch on the IPO date.
8. Lock-up period: the time period after an IPO when insiders at the new public company are restricted by the lead underwriter from selling their shares (usually lasts 180 days).

How long will it take to go public:

It takes an average of 3-12 months.

The Cost of going public:

The cost varies depending upon an individual company's history, size and complexity. The following figures are considered minimums.

- Legal - $50,000 to $200,000
- Accounting - $20,000 - $100,000
- Audit $30,000 - $200,00
- Printing - $20,000 -$80,000
- Other Fees $10,000 -$30,000

CLOSING THE BUSINESS

There are a number of reasons for closing a business:

Voluntary Dissolution: This is when you decide to close the business on your own.

Expiration of Existence: Some businesses have a specified term of existence in their articles of organization or incorporation. The business may file Articles of Amendment to extend its life otherwise it will cease to exist.

Involuntary Dissolution: If a corporation or limited liability company fails to file an Annual Report with the Secretary of State's office by the specified deadline, the Secretary of State, after sending a reminder, may dissolve the business. If you want to be "reinstated" after being involuntarily dissolved, you must file an Application for Reinstatement within a certain timeframe of dissolution.

You may also be forced to file for bankruptcy due to inability to repay debts. If you choose this option you can file under Chapter 7 or 11. Chapter 7 is a liquidation proceeding in which all assets, except for non-exempt assets are sold. Chapter 11 is a reorganization proceeding in which you can attempt to reorganize outstanding debts and continue operations of the business.

Suspension: Corporations that fail to file tax returns with the Department of Revenue for a specified number of years will be suspended or will forfeit their right to do business in the respective state. The corporation must pay its delinquent taxes within a certain timeframe of receiving a notice from the Department of Revenue or it will be dissolved or revoked by the Secretary of State.

Special Circumstances: Some types of businesses may dissolve under special circumstances. For example, a limited liability

company may dissolve if a member withdraws from the arrangement and the remaining members cannot agree on whether or not to continue being in business. Limited liability partnerships and limited partnerships will lose their liability protection unless they re-register every specified number of years.

Required Filings:
The steps for dissolving a business vary from state to state. Some

states have outlined specific procedures while others only require the filing of the appropriate form.

> Terminating a state corporation requires the filing of **Articles of Dissolution.**

> Terminating a foreign corporation requires the filing of a **Certificate of Withdrawal.**

> Termination of an LLC requires the filing of a **Certificate of Termination.**

STEPS FOR CLOSING YOUR BUSINESS

1. Check with the respective state for their outlined procedures and forms.
2. Obtain written permission for dissolution from all owners (stockholders) of your company (Statement of intent to Dissolve) prior to submitting a request for termination with your Secretary of State.
3. Notify employees (including contractors). Identify how you will handle termination of employee health insurance.
4. Identify and review open contracts (including leases). Determine if there are penalties for early cancellation. Identify the timeframe for cancellation notification.
5. Notify your customers and vendors.
6. Identify license and permits that may have to be terminated. There may be specific procedures for their termination. Check with the appropriate entity.

7. Get with your insurance service provider and ascertain what is the best way to terminate the business' insurance.
8. Identify how the company's assets will be handled. Will it be sold off or donated?
9. Identify any debts and determine how they will be paid. Provide written notice to creditors. Establish the priority for paying off debtors.

10. Pay outstanding state and federal taxes. Some states require that you obtain a "tax clearance certificate" before you can file your dissolution form. Don't forget to check the "final return" box on your final tax returns. See the IRS Checklist at **(http://www.irs.gov/businesses/small/article /0,,id=98703,00.html)**
11. Close accounts (bank, sales tax accounts, credit cards, etc.)
12. Submit your dissolution request with the respective state.
13. Maintain copies of business records for five years (required by the IRS).

Below is a list of resources where you can find liquidators. *Visit The Small Business Zone Web site* (**http://www.sbz1.com**) *for a more extensive list.*

DMOZ
http://www.dmoz.org/Business/Wholesale_Trade/Liquidat ors/
Directory of Liquidators.

Go Guides
http://www.goguides.org/topic/11681.html
Directory of Liquidators.

Wholesale Directory
http://www.wholesaledir.com/category/Liquidators/1
A Directory of liquidators. Search by product category.

CHAPTER 32

RESOURCES

These are a list of resources that you can employ to enhance your business.

Center for Women's Business Research
http://www.womensbusinessresearch.org
Provides information about women's businesses.

CWS Marketing Group
http://www.cwsmarketing.com
Market and sell personal and real property for the U.S. Treasury Department which includes the U. S. Customs Service, IRS, Secret Service and ATF. CWS through an online auction site.

Diversity Business Resources
https://www.diversitybusinessresources.com
Maintains a database of all minority owned businesses. Get listed for free in the database.

Export-Import Bank of the U.S.
http://www.exim.gov
The official export credit agency of the United States. They finance the export of goods and services to overseas markets. Ex-Im Bank provides working capital guarantees (pre-export financing), export credit insurance and loan guarantees and direct loans (buyer financing). No transaction is too large or too small.

General Services Administration Auctions
www.gsaauctions.gov
An online auction site where all agencies of the government post items for sale to the general public. Here you can find equipment ranging from computers to furniture.

GSA Schedule
http://www.gsa.gov/HP_02Cntrcts_schedules
If you want the federal government as you customer BE SURE TO GET LISTED IN THE GSA SCHEDULE. Under the GSA Schedules (also referred to as Multiple Award Schedules

and Federal Supply Schedules) Program, GSA establishes long-term government-wide contracts with commercial firms to provide access to over 10 million commercial supplies and services that can be ordered directly from GSA Schedule contractors or through the GSA Advantage online shopping and ordering system.

Merchant Barter Exchange
http://www.merchantsbarter.com
Trade goods and services with other businesses without the actual exchange of money.

MBDA (Minority Business Development Agency)
http://www.mbda.gov/?section_id=2
MBDA provides funding for a network of Minority Business Development Centers (MBDCs), Native American Business Development Centers (NABDCs) and Business Resource Centers (BRCs) located throughout the nation. These centers provide minority entrepreneurs with one-on-one assistance in writing business plans, marketing, management and technical assistance and financial planning to assure adequate financing for business ventures. The centers are staffed by business specialists who have the knowledge and practical experience needed to run successful and profitable businesses.

Diversity Business Resources
http://www.diversitybusinessresources.com
Maintains a database of all Minority Owned Businesses. Get listed for free in the Database.

NAA Live
http://www.naalive.com
An online auction site where you can buy all kinds of items, from furniture to farm equipment.

NFIB
http://www.nfib.com/page/home
The National Federation of Independent Business is the nation's leading small business advocacy association, with offices in all state capitals.

Overseas Private Investment Corp.
http://www.opic.gov
The Overseas Private Investment Corporation is a government entity that helps U.S. businesses invest overseas, fosters economic development in new and emerging markets and complements the private sector in managing risks associated with foreign direct investment.

Please Organize This
http://www.pleaseorganizethis.com
If you need help organizing and getting business tasks done: Web editing and formatting text and photos, managing computerize and manual filing systems, e-mail set-up, sorting and organizing, database sorting, creating and entry; designing flyers, brochures, business cards, administrative and clerical assistance.

SBA Women's Business Center
http://www.sba.gov/aboutsba/sbaprograms/onlinewbc/index.html
Provide contact information for Women's Business Centers by state. A national organization designed to help women start and grow their businesses.

The MWBE Directory
http://www.themwbedirectory.com
The source for looking up other MWBEs.

The Resource King
http://www.resourcekingintl.com
Identify, engage and increase the use of minority/Woman/ Veteran-Owned Enterprise (M.W.V.B.E.) firms on federal contracts.

Women-21
http://www.entrepreneurship.org/en/resource-center/women21gov.aspx
A program run by the Department of Labor and the SBA to promote the growth of women owned businesses.

WomenBiz
http://www.womenbiz.gov

A gateway for businesses owned by women to sell to the federal government.

<u>Vain Paradise</u>
http://www.vainparadise.com
A virtual assistant in Vain Paradise offers a broad range of professional administrative support services to busy entrepreneurs, startups and small companies at all levels of business development. From single projects to ongoing multi-level support.

CHAPTER 33

BUSINESS STATISTICS

Know more about your industry and your competition by doing market research. The resources below will provide access to business information.

Below is a list of sites that provide business statistics information. *Visit The Small Business Zone Web site (**http://www.sbz1.com**) for a more extensive list.*

BizStats
http://www.bizstats.com
BizStats is the home of free, accurate business statistics – well organized and easy to access. Provides detailed information by industry type. **COST: Free.**

Hoovers
http://www.hoovers.com/free/industries/
Find out who the competitors are in your industry from the Hoovers database of companies by industry. **COST: Free.**

IBS World
http://www.ibisworld.com/industry/home.aspx
See detailed statistics by industry type. If you're planning to get into a specific industry this is a good first source to do some research. **COST: Free**

CHAPTER 34

BUSINESS TERMS

Below is a list of resources where you can find business terms. *Visit The Small Business Zone Web site (**http://www.sbz1.com**) for a more extensive list.*

All Business
http://www.allbusiness.com/glossaries/business/4941806-1.html
A dictionary of business terms.

Wikipedia
http://en.wikipedia.org/wiki/List_of_business_and_finance_abbreviations
List of business abbreviations.

Princeton Hall
http://www.prenhall.com/glossary/a.html
Business terms in English and Spanish with audio.

Yahoo Small Business Dictionary
http://smallbusiness.yahoo.com/r-dictionary
Provides a list of business terms and allows you to conduct word searches.

CHAPTER 35

WOMEN BUSINESS RESOURCES

Women owned businesses are the fastest growing segment of new businesses. Hence, there is no surprise that there are many resources that cater to women owned businesses. Below is a list of resources that cater to women owned businesses. These organizations provide services such as networking opportunities, hold regular meetings, provide directory listing for your business, provide access to resources at discount prices, etc. Some organizations provide free membership while others require you to pay a membership fee. You can determine which one is best for you by examining what they have to offer.

Below is a short list of resources that are dedicated to serving women entrepreneurs. *Visit The Small Business Zone Web site (**http://www.sbz1.com**) for a more extensive list.*

Alliance of Women Entrepreneurs
http://www.winwomen.org
AWE is the Greater Philadelphia region's only organization specifically for women who are leaders of and investors in high-growth businesses. AWE promotes the expansion of women-led and women-owned businesses through education, networking, mentoring, and exposure to investment resources.

Black Business Women Online
http://mybbwo.com
Promote your business and network with over 8,000 members. Post photos & Videos. Promote and find events. Join blogs. There is a one-time fee of $25.00.

Chicago Women Entrepreneur Network
http://www.meetup.com/chicago-women-entrepreneurs/
Whether you're starting your business or a seasoned business owner, we All have something to contribute! Let's build this

network together. Consistency is key. We'll have regular monthly networking sessions, special events, and expos designed for the women entrepreneur.

Circle of Moms
http://www.circleofmoms.com/entrepreneur-moms/Northern-Colorado-Women-Entrepreneurs-Network-299795

A Northern Colorado Women Entrepreneurs Network. A local group in NoCo to get together with other like-minded women, swap business cards, network, and brainstorm. meet physically on the 3rd Thursday of each month at a local restaurant.

Columbus area women's business council
http://www.ywcacolumbus.org/site/PageServer?pagename=programs_leadershiplunch

Fostering opportunities for women in Central Ohio. Conducts leadership luncheons and Women to Women networking events.

Community of Women Entrepreneurs
http://www.reformsnetwork.org/women/

The Community of Women Entrepreneurs shares ideas, experiences, best practices, and resources to empower women economically and politically. Members of this community are leading entrepreneurs and business advocates who share their knowledge and in return receive fresh ideas from their peers.

Enterprising Women's Magazine
http://enterprisingwomen.com/

A magazine for Women Business Owners. Provides news and interviews on women owned businesses.

Entrepreneur Women's Network
http://www.ewn-ct.org/

Provide information, activities, and support that will help EWN members grow their businesses and run their businesses more effectively.

CHAPTER 36

SMALL BUSINESS SCAMS

Small businesses are often targeted by scammers. These scams come in all forms. Their aim is to steal you of your products and services or money. Scammers assume that Small Business owners are vulnerable to scams because they are eager to make a profit and don't pay attention to detail as they should, or they are not knowledgeable of the methods used to defraud them. Scams successfully perpetrated on businesses (especially small businesses) can lead to the demise of a business. It is very advisable for a small business owner to become knowledgeable of the different ways they can be scammed and the measures they need to take to avoid being scammed.

Below is a short list of scams aimed at small businesses. *Visit The Small Business Zone Web site (**http://www.sbz1.com**) for a more extensive list.*

1. The Overpayment Approach:
This is when individual intending to rip you off order your product or service and pay you with a check to cover the cost. But, instead of writing the check for the exact amount they write the check for more than what it cost (let's say $200 more). You being the nice person that you are, write them a check for the over paid amount. Only later you find out that their check was from a bank account that had been closed years earlier. Not only did they get your product or service for free, they also get some cash out of it. Perpetrators of this scheme will often emphasize the need for the item in a hurry, prompting haste over sound judgment.

Protect your business:
    1. Return overpaid checks immediately, and ask for a check in the proper amount.
    2. Never send products or refunds to a first-time buyer until their check has cleared the bank.

2. Valuation Fraud:
"The business sends faxes asking if you're interested in selling your

business, "If you want to sell your business, they claim they'll find buyers interested in your company. You send a fax back, and they send someone to come out to speak with you. After that, you pay several thousand dollars in advance to have a valuation done to determine what your business is worth. After you've paid, they disappear,"

Protect your business:
Always check a company's references before pre-paying for any services.

3. Government Compliance:
One company played on fear of the government by sending out unsolicited faxes and direct mail in an attempt to sell their grossly overpriced posters used for displaying government regulations to employees. These contained information that must be posted in offices stating the correct minimum wage and other state and federal requirements. Such companies use scare tactics such as, "if your company does not display this compliance poster, it will face a fine of $5,000. Another scare tactic is the claim that they have insurance against errors in the posters.

Protect your business:
1. You can get this for free. It is also available at cost for less than $100.
2. You will not be fined for errors on the poster.

APPENDIX A

A SIMPLE PLAN

It is not necessary to have a formal business plan to go into business (formal business plans for the most part are used to obtain financing from Venture Capitalists or other financial institutions). Think of a simple plan as a roadmap that shows the major roadways and key features as opposed to the formal business plan that shows street level details.

To arrive at your **simple plan** engage in some **backwards planning** by answering a few questions. **Backwards planning** is starting at the end and working your way back to the beginning. Start with outlining what it is that you want to achieve and working step-by-step back to the beginning. Answer the questions below to derive at a simple plan.

1. What is the objective (goal)?

Be very specific about your goals. Examples include:

- Generate $1,000,000 in revenues annually from selling widget "A" by the second year of operations. In order to accomplish this I must sell 2,604 widgets every month at a price of $32.00 each.
- Gain 1,000,000 customers in the first year of operations. In order to accomplish this I must sign-up 83,333 new customers every month.
- Maintain 90% occupancy rate by the third year of operations. In order to accomplish this I must sign up 5 new tenants every month on a two-year lease.

2. How would you price your product/service; how many units must sell per month and at what price?

- You need to know what the industry standard for pricing range for your product/service is. Will the market bear the price you are asking for?

- What are your competitors charging for the same product/service?
- Your product should be price as a multiple of production cost (e.g. 4 x production cost; in other words if production cost is $8, then 4 x $8= $32).
- Will the price you charge give you a big enough profit margin to cover for other expenses such as overhead costs and other unforeseen expenses?
- What is the amount of items I have to sell each month in order to meet my objective?

3. Who is your target audience?

- Pick your target audience based on demographic factors such as age, sex, income levels, education levels, location, etc.
- When you pick a demographic be very specific. This will help you focus your resources and message.

4. How would you market to them and what will it cost?

- There are many ways you can market to your target audience. The question is which route is the most effective in terms of reaching your target audience without busting your budget.
- Be very specific about which marketing methods you will use and what it will cost for each. For example:
  - Place 2"x 4" newspaper ads in mid-west newspapers = $450 per month
  - Street teams to hand flyers in busy downtown areas = $500 per month
  - Mail 1,000 postcards a month to local residents = $250 per month

5. How would you deliver the product/service?

- Will the product be sold at a store front shop where customers have to walk in and make the purchase?
- Will it be sold over the Internet where customers place orders on the Web and the product is then mail to them from a warehouse location? ***What is the shipping cost?*** Will the shipping cost be included in the price?
- Will it be sold through third parties such as affiliates? If so what percentage of the profits you have to give up?
- Is your method the most effective way to sell the product? Is it increasing or decreasing the cost of doing business? Does it pose any risks that could negatively impact the business?

6. What is the startup cost?

- What does it cost for the following:
  - Register the business
  - Register the domain name
  - Web site setup
  - Rent an office
  - Office furniture and supplies
  - Production equipment
  - Initial production supplies
  - Labor cost
  - Insurance coverage
  - Legal fees
  - Business cards
  - Storage
  - Business license fee, etc.

7. What is the production/service delivery cost?

- How much does it cost to produce the item or deliver the service? If you paid $1,000 for supplies

needed to make widget "A," but you can only
produce 100 widget "A's" from those supplies, then
the cost per widget "A" is $10.

- The question you should be asking yourself at this
point is is there other supply sources you can use
that will provide you the same supplies at a reduced
rate.

8. What will the overhead cost be?

Overhead costs are recurring that you pay every month.
Consider the following overhead items and their cost:

- Office rent
- Electricity
- Phone service
- Internet service
- Cost of labor
- Transportation
- Etc.

9. How long does it take to produce an item and what will it take to produce the desired amount in the desired timeframe?

You have identified above how many items you need to sell every
month. Now you need to identify what it will take to produce that
number of items every month.

If it takes 20 minutes to produce one widget "A" using one
machine, and one machine can produce 72 widget "A's" in 24
hours. Then in 24 hours I could produce 144 widget "A's"
utilizing two machines.

10. Where will you obtain the raw materials for the product?

- Consider the difference between obtaining your
supplies domestically (in country) and from overseas.
- Prices may be slightly higher when buying
domestically. However, when buying from overseas

there are customs fees and transportation costs that will add to the overall price of the supplies.
- Consider the time it takes to receive a shipment from overseas from the moment you place the order.
- Consider unforeseen delays in the supply chain if buying from overseas. This could slow production and drive up the cost of production.
- Consider the ramification if an overseas supplier takes your money and does not deliver the product. What legal recourse will you have?
- Consider the ramification if an overseas supplier supplied you with raw materials that does not meet federal safety standards.

11. How is the product/service being produced (in-house/outsource)?

- Will you produce the product in-house or will you outsource it. Do the research to determine which one is cheaper.
- If you want to protect the secrecy of the product until you bring it to market outsourcing may not be a good deal.
- Outsourcing sometimes requires you to put forth more money upfront because producers want you to buy certain minimum quantities. This may not fit into your budget.

12. What financing would you need and where will you get it from?

- What is the total sum of money you will need? How much of it you can self-finance, and how much of it will require other sources of financing?
- Consider the sources of financing:
  - Family
  - Friends
  - Banks
  - Venture Capitalists
  - Angel Investors

- Peer-to-Peer lending

13. What market forces could negatively impact the business?

Consider how the following could negatively impact the business and what you can do to mitigate them.

- *Recession:* A slow-down in the economy would force consumers to change their buying habits and put off buying your product/service.
- *Laws:* Could federal or state laws be passed that would impact your product. For example, a new safety standard that could force you to re-engineer your product.
- *Counterfeit:* Could the market be flooded with counterfeit items of your product. How would you fight that?
- *Legal:* Are there safety risks with your product that has the potential for a lawsuit. Could someone sue you for infringement of their patent?

APPENDIX B

LIST OF STATES WEB SITES WHERE YOU CAN INCORPORATE YOUR BUSINESS.

Alabama: [$40]
http://www.sos.state.al.us/businessServices/corporations.aspx
Alaska: [$250.00]
http://www.dced.state.ak.us/occ/home.htm
Arizona: [$60]
http://www.cc.state.az.us/Divisions/Corporations/
Arkansas: [$50]
http://www.sos.arkansas.gov/corp_ucc_online_services.html
California: [$100]
http://www.sos.ca.gov/business/forms.htm
Colorado: [$50]
http://www.sos.state.co.us/pubs/business/main.htm
Connecticut: [$200]
http://www.sots.ct.gov/sots/site/default.asp
Delaware: [$89]
https://sos-res.state.de.us/tin/GINameSearch.jsp
Florida: [$35]
http://www.sunbiz.org/
Georgia: [$100]
http://sos.georgia.gov/corporations/
Hawaii: [$50]
http://www.ehawaii.gov/dakine/index.html
Idaho:[$100-$120]
https://labor.idaho.gov/applications/ibrs/ibr.aspx
Illinois: [$150]
http://www.cyberdriveillinois.com/departments/business_services/home.html
Indiana: [$90]
http://www.in.gov/sos/business/
Iowa: [$50]
http://www.iowalifechanging.com/business/startup.aspx
Kansas: [$90]
http://www.kansas.gov/business/
Kentucky: [$50]
http://www.sos.ky.gov/business/

Louisiana: [$60]
http://www.sos.louisiana.gov/tabid/115/Default.aspx
Maine: [$145]
http://www.maine.gov/portal/business/
Maryland: [$120]
http://blis.choosemaryland.org/BusinessStartup.aspx
Massachusetts: [$275]
http://www.sec.state.ma.us/cor/coridx.htm
Michigan: [$60]
http://www.michigan.gov/business/0,1607,7-255-52649---
,00.html
Minnesota: [$160]
http://www.sos.state.mn.us/home/index.asp?page=3
Missouri: [$58]
http://www.business.mo.gov/
Mississippi: [$50]
http://www.sos.state.ms.us/busserv/corporations.asp
Montana: [$70]
http://mt.gov/business.asp
Nebraska: [$60]
http://www.sos.state.ne.us/business/
Nevada: [$75]
http://sos.state.nv.us/business/
New Hampshire: [$100]
http://www.nh.gov/business/index.html
New Jersey: [$125]
http://www.state.nj.us/njbusiness/starting/
New Mexico: [$100]
http://www.sos.state.nm.us/sos-corp.html
New York: [$135]
http://www.dos.state.ny.us/corp/filing.html
North Carolina: [$125]
http://www.secretary.state.nc.us/Corporations/
North Dakota: [$100]
http://www.nd.gov/businessreg/register/index.html
Oregon: [$50]
http://www.filinginoregon.com/
Oklahoma: [$50]
http://www.sos.state.ok.us/business/business_filing.htm
Ohio: [$125]
http://www.sos.state.oh.us/SOS/businessServices.aspx

Pennsylvania: [$125]
http://www.dos.state.pa.us/corps/site/default.asp
Rhode Island: [$230]
https://www.ri.gov/taxation/BAR/
South Carolina: [$110]
http://www.sc.gov/Portal/Category/BUSINESS_TOP
South Dakota: [$150]
http://sdsos.gov/busineservices/busineservices_overview.shtm
Tennessee: [$100]
http://www.tennessee.gov/sos/bus_svc/index.htm
Texas: [$300]
http://www.sos.state.tx.us/corp/index.shtml
Utah: [$52]
http://www.utah.gov/services/business.html
Vermont: [$75]
http://www.sec.state.vt.us/corps/corpindex.htm
Virginia: [$75]
http://www.virginia.gov/cmsportal3/business_4096/index.htmll
Washington: [$180]
http://www.secstate.wa.gov/corps/registration_requirements.aspx
West Virginia: [$50]
http://www.wv.gov/business/Pages/default.aspx
Wisconsin: [$100]
http://www.wisconsin.gov/state/core/business.html
Wyoming: [$100]
http://soswy.state.wy.us/Business/Business.aspx

APPENDIX C

STATES' WEB SITES FOR SALES TAX ID

Alabama
http://www.revenue.alabama.gov/incometax/icindex.cfm
Alaska [no sales tax]
http://www.tax.alaska.gov/programs/index.aspx
Arizona
https://www.aztaxes.gov
Arkansas
http://www.state.ar.us/dfa/dfa_taxes.html
California
http://taxes.ca.gov/
Colorado
http://www.revenue.state.co.us/TPS_Dir/wrap.asp?incl=business
es
Connecticut
http://www.ct.gov/drs/taxonomy/drs_taxonomy.asp?DLN=4082
3&drsNav=|40823|
Delaware
http://www.ct.gov/drs/cwp/view.asp?a=1509&q=266240
Florida
http://dor.myflorida.com/dor/eservices/apps/register/
Georgia
http://www.etax.dor.ga.gov/CorpTax_TSD.aspx
Hawaii
http://www.state.hi.us/tax/tax.html
Idaho
http://tax.idaho.gov/answers_Sales_tax.htm#5
Illinois
http://www.revenue.state.il.us/Businesses/
Indiana
http://www.in.gov/dor/3963.htm
Iowa

https://www.idr.iowa.gov/CBA/start.asp

Kansas

http://www.ksrevenue.org/business.htm

Kentucky

http://www.thinkkentucky.com/KYEDC/biztax.aspx

Louisiana

http://www.revenue.louisiana.gov/sections/business/sales.aspx

Maine

http://www.maine.gov/portal/business/taxes.html

Maryland

http://business.marylandtaxes.com/taxinfo/salesanduse/default.asp

Massachusetts

https://wfb.dor.state.ma.us/webfile/business/Public/Webforms/
Login/Login.aspx

Michigan

http://www.michigan.gov/taxes

Minnesota

http://www.taxes.state.mn.us/business_taxpayers/index.shtml

Mississippi

http://www.mstc.state.ms.us/

Missouri

http://dor.mo.gov/tax/business/

Montana

http://mt.gov/revenue/

Nebraska

http://www.revenue.state.ne.us/business/business.htm

New Hampshire [does not have general sales tax]

http://www.nh.gov/revenue/

Nevada

http://tax.state.nv.us/

New Jersey

https://www.state.nj.us/cgi-bin/treasury/revenue/dcr/filing/page1.cgi

New Mexico

http://www.tax.state.nm.us/BizPge.htm

New York

http://www.tax.state.ny.us/sbc/sell.htm

North Dakot

http://www.nd.gov/businessreg/tax/index.html

North Carolina

http://www.dor.state.nc.us/downloads/sales.html

Ohio

http://tax.ohio.gov/divisions/sales_and_use/license.stm

Oklahoma

http://www.tax.ok.gov/btforms.html

Oregon [no sales & use tax]

http://oregon.gov/DOR/salestax.shtml

Pennsylvania

http://www.pa100.state.pa.us/

Rhode Island

http://www.tax.ri.gov/taxforms/sales_excise/sales_use.php

South Carolina

http://www.sctax.org/Forms+and+Instructions/businessRegistration/default.htm

South Dakota

http://www.state.sd.us/drr2/businesstax/bustax.htm

Tennessee

http://www.tennesseeanytime.org/bizreg/

Texas

http://www.cpa.state.tx.us/taxpermit/

Utah

http://www.tax.utah.gov/business/registration.html#tc69

Vermont

http://www.state.vt.us/tax/businessstarting.shtml

Virginia

http://www.tax.virginia.gov/

Washington

http://dor.wa.gov/content/doingbusiness/

West Virginia

http://www.state.wv.us/taxrev/uploads/busapp.pdf

Wisconsin

http://www.dor.state.wi.us/forms/sales/index.html

Wyoming

http://revenue.state.wy.us/PortalVBVS/DesktopDefault.aspx?tabindex=2&tabid=9

APPENDIX D

STATE WORKPLACE SAFETY REQUIREMENTS

Alabama
http://dir.alabama.gov/docs/doc_type.aspx?id=2
Alaska
http://www.labor.state.ak.us/lss/posters.htm
Arizona
http://az.gov/webapp/portal/displaycontent.jsp?id=1645
Arkansas
http://www.accessarkansas.org/labor/pdf/required_postings2002.
pdf
California
http://www.dir.ca.gov/dlse/RequiredPosters.pdf
Colorado
http://www.coworkforce.com/LAB/PostingRequirements.pdf
Connecticut
http://www.ctdol.state.ct.us/wgwkstnd/posters.htm
Delaware
https://onestop.delaware.gov/osbrlpublic/Home.jsp
Florida
http://www.floridajobs.org/workforce/posters.html
Georgia
http://www.dol.state.ga.us/em/required_posters.htm
Hawaii
http://hawaii.gov/labor/poster_2006.shtml
Idaho
http://labor.idaho.gov/dnn/idl/Businesses/EmploymentServices
/FormsPosters/tabid/649/Default.aspx
Illinois
http://www.state.il.us/agency/idol/Posters/poster.htm
Indiana
http://www.in.gov/wcb/2371.htm
Iowa
http://www.iowaworkforce.org/labor/forms.htm
Kansas

http://www.dol.ks.gov/es/html/posters_dbr.html
Kentucky
http://revenue.ky.gov/business/
Louisiana
http://laborlawposters.gov-docs.com/louisiana/index.php
Maine
http://www.maine.gov/labor/posters/
Maryland
http://www.dllr.state.md.us/oeope/poster.shtml
Massachusetts
http://www.mass.gov/ [then click on the BUSINESS tab, then on
WORKPLACE & EMPLOYEES, then Poster Requirements
Michigan
http://www.michigan.gov/dleg/0,1607,7-154-27673-42129--
,00.html
Minnesota
http://www.dli.mn.gov/LS/Posters.asp
Mississippi
http://www.mwcc.state.ms.us/INFO/_posters.asp
Missouri
http://www.dolir.mo.gov/posters2.htm
Montana
http://wsd.dli.mt.gov/service/posters.asp
Nebraska
http://www.dol.nebraska.gov/nwd/center.cfm?PRICAT=2&SUB
CAT=5F
Nevada
http://www.nsbdc.org/toolbox/tools/pdfs/Required_Posters.pdf
New Hampshire
http://www.labor.state.nh.us/mandatory_posters.asp
New Jersey
http://lwd.dol.state.nj.us/labor/employer/content/employerpacke
tforms.html
New Mexico
http://www.dws.state.nm.us/dws-posters.html
New York
http://www.labor.state.ny.us/workerprotection/laborstandards/e
mployer/posters.shtm
North Carolina
http://www.nclabor.com/pubs.htm
North Dakota

http://www.nd.gov/labor/publications/posters.html
Ohio
http://das.ohio.gov/hrd/laborlawposters.html
Oklahoma
http://www.ok.gov/odol/Wage_and_Hour/Worplace_posters.html
Oregon
http://www.boli.state.or.us/BOLI/CRD/C_Postings.shtml
Pennsylvania
http://www.dli.state.pa.us/landi/cwp/view.asp?a=354&q=63528
Rhode Island
http://www.dlt.ri.gov/lmi/business/post.htm
South Carolina
http://www.llr.state.sc.us/aboutus/index.asp?file=DOPI.HTM
South Dakota
http://dol.sd.gov/employerserv/postingrequirements.aspx
Tennessee
http://www.state.tn.us/labor-wfd/poster.htm
Texas
http://www.texasworkforce.org/ui/lablaw/posters.html
Utah
http://laborcommission.utah.gov/AdministrativeServices/RequiredPosters.html
Vermont
http://www.labor.vermont.gov/FormsPublications/WageHourFormsandPublications/tabid/128/Default.aspx/
Virginia
http://www.doli.virginia.gov/publications/required_posters.html
Washington
http://www.lni.wa.gov/ipub/101-054-000.pdf
West Virginia
http://www.state.wv.us/admin/personnel/emprel/posters/posreqstate.pdf
Wisconsin
http://www.dwd.state.wi.us/dwd/posters.htm
Wyoming
http://wydoe.state.wy.us/doe.asp?ID=576

APPENDIX E

STATE CORPORATE TAX RATES

(As of the published date of this book)

State	Tax Rates	Federal Tax Deductible
ALABAMA	6.5	
ALASKA	1.0 - 9.4	
ARIZONA	6.968	
ARKANSAS	1.0 - 6.5	
CALIFORNIA	8.84	
COLORADO	4.63	
CONNECTICUT	7.5	
DELAWARE	8.7	
FLORIDA	5.5	
GEORGIA	6.0	
HAWAII	4.4 - 6.4	
IDAHO	7.6	
ILLINOIS	7.3	
INDIANA	8.5	
IOWA	6.0 - 12.0	50%
KANSAS	4.0 – 7.05	
KENTUCKY	4.0 - 6.0	
LOUISIANA	4.0 - 8.0	
MAINE	3.5 - 8.93	
MARYLAND	8.25	
MASSACHUSETTS	8.8	
MICHIGAN	4.95	
MINNESOTA	9.8	
MISSISSIPPI	3.0 - 5.0	
MISSOURI	6.25	50%
MONTANA	6.75	

NEBRASKA	5.58 - 7.81	
NEVADA	**0**	
NEW HAMPSHIRE	8.5	
NEW JERSEY	9.0	
NEW MEXICO	4.8 - 7.6	
NEW YORK	7.1	
NORTH CAROLINA	6.9	
NORTH DAKOTA	2.6 - 6.5	
OHIO	0.26	
OKLAHOMA	6.0	
OREGON	6.6	
PENNSYLVANIA	9.99	
RHODE ISLAND	9.0	
SOUTH CAROLINA	5.0	
SOUTH DAKOTA	**0**	
TENNESSEE	6.5	
TEXAS	**0**	
UTAH	5.0	
VERMONT (b)	6.0 - 8.5	
VIRGINIA	6.0	
WASHINGTON	**0**	
WEST VIRGINIA	8.5	
WISCONSIN	7.9	
WYOMING	**0**	
DIST. OF COLUMBIA	9.975	

APPENDIX F

TOP 20 BANKS

The top 20 banks that support small business banking is listed below. Their ranking is based on analysis on the following categories:

Minimum Balance Requirement: Some banks have a "no minimum balance requirement" for the life of the account while others require a minimum after the first year. The "no minimum balance requirement" is the preferred method. Most small business owners have to self-finance their venture and hence capital reserves are low. Charging them a fee on top of that to have a bank account is not supportive.

Online Banking: Some banks provide free online banking while others charge a fee for the service. A cost of $0.0 is the preferred fee for this service. Since banks already benefit from charging fees in other areas.

Monthly Fees: Some banks charge no monthly fees while others charge a flat fee based on the minimum monthly balance for business accounts. Some banks will charge no monthly fee if you have at least one monthly transaction on your account. The lower the fee the better.

Minimum amount to open an Account: Some banks do not require a deposit in order to open an account. Others do require a small amount to open an account while others require thousands of dollars. This minimum amount required to open an account should not exceed $25.00. Keep in mind that once you open an account some banks will charge fees for maintaining monthly minimums.

Paperwork required for opening an account: All banks listed require the minimum amount of paperwork to open an account.

These banks also offer Overdraft Protection, Credit Cards, Debit Cards, Small Business Loans.

#	Bank	Minimum To Open an Account
1	Bankers Trust	$1.00
2	Northrim Bank	$1.00
3	People's Bank	$1.00
4	PNC Bank	$1.00
5	U.S. Bank	$1.00
6	Fifth Third Bank	$1.00
7	Bank of Elk River	$25.00
8	Marine Bank	$100.00
9	First Citizens Bank	$1.00
10	Country Club Bank of Kansas City	$1.00
11	First Interstate Bank	$1.00
12	Grand Bank	$1.00
13	Sun Trust Bank	$1.00
14	First Commercial Bank	$1.00
15	BBVA Compass Bank	$100.00
16	Bank United	$100.00
17	Wells Fargo Bank	$100.00
18	Regions Bank	$1.00
19	Bank of America	$0.00
20	Chase Bank	$25.00

APPENDIX G

STATE DATABASES

Alabama
http://www.sos.state.al.us/BusinessServices/Default.aspx
Alaska
https://myalaska.state.ak.us/business/soskb/csearch.asp
Arizona
http://starpas.azcc.gov/scripts/cgiip.exe/WService=wsbroker1/main.p
Arkansas
http://www.sosweb.state.ar.us/corps/index.html
California
http://kepler.sos.ca.gov/list.html
Colorado
http://www.sos.state.co.us/biz/BusinessEntityCriteriaExt.do
Connecticut
http://www.concord-sots.ct.gov/CONCORD/index.jsp
Delaware
http://www.corp.delaware.gov/directweb.shtml
Florida
http://www.sunbiz.org/search.html
Georgia
http://corp.sos.state.ga.us/corp/soskb/CSearch.asp
Hawaii
http://hbe.ehawaii.gov/documents/search.html
Idaho
http://www.accessidaho.org/public/sos/corp/search.html?ScriptForm.startstep=crit
Illinois
http://www.ilsos.gov/corporatellc/
Indiana
https://secure.in.gov/sos/bus_service/online_corps/name_search.aspx
Iowa
http://www.sos.state.ia.us/search/corp/corp_search.asp
Kansas
http://www.accesskansas.org/srv-corporations/search.do
Kentucky

http://apps.sos.ky.gov/business/obdb/default.aspx
Louisiana
http://www400.sos.louisiana.gov/app1/paygate/crpinq.jsp
Maine
https://icrs.informe.org/nei-sos-icrs/ICRS;jsessionid=FD0961D3872C121592F00F953CD47CEE?MainPage=x
Maryland
http://sdatcert3.resiusa.org/UCC-Charter/CharterSearch_f.aspx
Massachusetts
http://corp.sec.state.ma.us/corp/corpsearch/corpsearchinput.asp
Michigan
http://www.dleg.state.mi.us/bcs_corp/sr_corp.asp
Minnesota
http://da.sos.state.mn.us/minnesota/corp_inquiry-find.asp?:Norder_item_type_id=10
Missouri
https://www.sos.mo.gov/BusinessEntity/soskb/csearch.asp
Mississippi
https://business.sos.state.ms.us/corp/soskb/csearch.asp
Montana
http://app.mt.gov/bes/
Nebraska
http://www.sos.ne.gov/business/corp_serv/
Nevada
https://esos.state.nv.us/SOSServices/AnonymousAccess/CorpSearch/CorpSearch.aspx
New Hampshire
https://www.sos.nh.gov/corporate/soskb/csearch.asp
New Jersey
https://accessnet.state.nj.us/error.asp
New Mexico
http://www.nmprc.state.nm.us/cii.htm
New York
http://appsext8.dos.state.ny.us/corp_public/CORPSEARCH.ENTITY_SEARCH_ENTRY
North Carolina
http://www.secretary.state.nc.us/corporations/CSearch.aspx
North Dakota
https://secure.apps.state.nd.us/sc/busnsrch/busnSearch.htm

Ohio
http://www.sos.state.oh.us/SOS/about/dutiesResponsibilities/databases.aspx
Oklahoma
https://www.sooneraccess.state.ok.us/corp_inquiry/corp_inquiry-find.asp?:Norder_item_type_id=22
Oregon
http://egov.sos.state.or.us/br/pkg_web_name_srch_inq.login
Pennsylvania
http://www.corporations.state.pa.us/corp/soskb/csearch.asp?corpsNav=|
Rhode Island
http://ucc.state.ri.us/CorpSearch/CorpSearchInput.asp
South Carolina
http://www.scsos.com/corp_search.htm
South Dakota
http://www.sdsos.gov/busineservices/corporations.shtm
Tennessee
http://www.tennesseeanytime.org/soscorp/
Texas
http://ecpa.cpa.state.tx.us/coa/Index.html
Utah
https://secure.utah.gov/bes/action/index
Vermont
http://www.sec.state.vt.us/seek/corpbrow.htm
Virginia
http://www.scc.virginia.gov/clk/bussrch.aspx
Washington
http://www.secstate.wa.gov/corps/
West Virginia
http://www.wvsos.com/wvcorporations/
Wisconsin
http://www.wdfi.org/apps/CorpSearch/Search.aspx
Wyoming
https://wyobiz.wy.gov/

INDEX

www.ingramcontent.com/pod-product-compliance
Lightning Source LLC
Chambersburg PA
CBHW070524200326
41519CB00013B/2923